CREEDS AND CREDIBILITY

By

C. B. ARMSTRONG

Canon and Vice-Dean of Worcester

LONDON

A. R. MOWBRAY & CO LTD

Printed in Great Britain by
Alden & Mowbray Ltd
at the Alden Press, Oxford

SBN 264 65584 2

First Published in 1969

To HESTER

AUTHOR'S FOREWORD

To publish one more work on theology would be impertinent if it had not a definite purpose. This is written for the many intelligent churchmen and churchwomen of today who have serious intellectual difficulties in accepting the creeds of orthodoxy in their literal meaning, while personally desiring the commitment of faith. They find a certain insincerity in asserting credal beliefs simply as matters of faith without intellectual conviction of their truth; and in some cases the feeling is so strong that sincerity is preferred to adherence.

For their comfort this book is written. Its thesis is briefly that God's revelation of himself has been progressive in history; that man's understanding of it has always been expressed through the thought-background of the ages in which it was received. That therefore, because the revelation has been historical, a certain divergence has grown between the truth as intellectually understood at various periods and the symbolic 'schemata' into which they were translated for the religious of the day.

A commitment of faith is therefore possible to the structure of so-called orthodoxy, historically built and historically effective at all times, even though intellectual discernment of the underlying truths must change with changing ages so far as thought can achieve it.

There is a gulf which is widening between faith and belief; and yet, as I have tried to show, new intellectual understanding of God's revelations need not inhibit personal commitment to the religious drama of God's dealings with man, in which they have found wonderful expression.

C.B.A.

CONTENTS

PART ONE

6. SCIENTISM 39

Scientism has vast utilitarian possibilities, but can point to no spiritual and few moral values. It accepts the dictation of physical facts but must be silent on what we most want to know. Much of what makes life worth living—religion, art, music, poetry and love are beyond its scope.

7. PERSONAL THINKING 43

The personality of the thinker is shown to produce marked effects on the character of his thought. His feelings, his will, his tastes and his situation colour his views. Our thought is limited by our human situation, our powers, and our psychological character, and cannot be complete in itself.

8. HUMAN THOUGHT IN GENERAL 50

A summary of this review shows that human thinking is always subject to limitations. It must be guarded by reason from reliance on insights and opinions. It is always about presented objects, and is always through a personal thought-background. For Christians this background is belief in God and the object in general is his creation and man in particular.

9. PRESUPPOSITIONS OF THIS APPROACH 54

An attempt is made to describe the thought-background of a present-day Christian, whose religious outlook is affected by the spirit of our times. It is the glass through which a non-theological thinker tries to survey his faith and his problems. But some of the scheme which is officially presented by the Church is antiquated, and a measure of reconstruction seems inevitable.

PART TWO

PROLOGUE 59

A caution against obscurantism or excessive dogmatism. If central Christian beliefs can be made more livable rationally by interpretation the gain will be far greater than the loss of those who hold bravely to the whole dogmatic tradition in spite of its difficulties. Faith must have reasonable as well as factual grounds. If a more comprehensible explanation leaves the belief unaltered it is to be preferred. Revelation has been given to men of many periods, and has been expressed by them in the terms of their age which are not necessarily for all time.

1. THE NEW TESTAMENT 63

The old truths of the revelation to the Hebrews had been expressed in the terms of various periods. The new truth of Jesus Christ's revelation of God had at first to wear Jewish dress, and later to put on a further adornment of Christian symbols. Some legendary accretions were inevitable during the 'silent years'. The growth of truth in symbolic form is multifarious, and even fluctuant. But the living Person who shines through the New Testament is immune to critical dissection.

2. THE BEING OF GOD 68

To know God is to experience personal life in its highest quality. He is utterly real, but the experience of him is primarily subjective. Only secondarily do we rationally know him as objective. Objectivity lessens his interpersonal reality. Reasons why he is not merely personal but a supreme Person.

3. THE HOLY TRINITY. 73

God is known to us in three ways each of which is highly personal. But the theology of three hypostases in one *ousia* is out-dated and illogical. The error is due to a false concept of substance, plus a certainty of God as active in three ways among Christians, in spite of their commitments to Jewish monotheism. All depends on separating what should never have been divided.

4. CREATION 77

Neither science nor religion can pronounce on the beginning of things. We can only say 'the earth is the Lord's and the fulness thereof' as an ontological statement. The being of things as well as their values have their ground in God. Although 'creation out of nothing' is logically impossible and we must say simply that creation depends on God, we cannot regard it as a projection of his imagination. The presuppositions of theology are not time, space and matter. Various theories examined. Energy, particularly the energy expressed physically through living organisms, may provide a clue.

5. INCARNATION 85

Christianity, unlike other religions, is centred on God incarnate. Conviction of his divinity may well have created the legends of his birth. We can believe that 'in him dwelt the fulness of the Godhead bodily' and that 'the Word was made flesh' on the lines of complete self-dedication of Jesus to God, and complete possession of him by the divine Spirit. 'God was in Christ' means complete spiritual unity. God as person was in Christ as person. Errors of Christology. Adoptionism need not be heretical in a revised form.

Note to Chapter 5. ADOPTIONISM IN THE NEW TESTAMENT 89

6. THE ATONEMENT 94

Experience and conviction of its truth is firm in Christians: theories of how it is possible give partial aspects, each of which has some value and presents some difficulties. The sacrificial theory and its links with the O.T. The Pauline explanation suggested by contemporary religious speculation. Other theories are less adequate. A revelatory theory based on the Incarnation is suggested. It is not purely exemplary because it reveals as a fact the forgiving love of God.

7. THE RESURRECTION 101

A summary of the evidence and of various explanations. If, as seems most probable, its factuality must be accepted, an explanation based on love as the recreative power of the future life is suggested.

8. THE HOLY GHOST 108

Is he to be regarded as a co-equal and separate person in the Godhead? Some uncertainty in the early Church: indication of this in sacramental theology: and in the constructive period before the creed of Constantinople and Leo's Tome. A conception of God as living personal spirit might have removed some difficulties created by the early concepts of substance.

9. THE CHURCH 113

It defies definition. It exists to continue the work of Christ in communion with him, in worship, in teaching and service to mankind, in witness and evangelization. Why an institutional church is necessary: reform must not forget the historical perspective. Certain modifications may well be necessary, in the formulation of doctrine, in greater charity of moral teaching, and in purging of organizational machinery.

10. SOTERIOLOGY 123

The concept of salvation has changed with changing social conditions. But its main emphases are still twofold, salvation from sin and salvation from 'lostness'. The Church's remedies for the former are repentance and forgiveness: for lostness she proclaims Christ as the way, the truth and the life, and seeks to work out its consequences in society. The Christian experience of forgiveness.

11. SACRAMENTS 129

The Christian tries to live at a spiritual level which is not that of society in general. He tries to realize the city of God in the cities of man: and for this task he needs spiritual strength and refreshment sacramentally conveyed. We enter into a symbolism by which the spiritual is conveyed to the social level, and the sacraments, charged with power from on high, are our means of translating it into active life. Sacraments are, as it were, a bridge between the eternal and the temporal. They become active in and through the Church for the world.

12. THE LAST THINGS 135

Here our inheritance of knowledge from the New Testament is least satisfactory. It is coloured by apocalyptic of the past, and the prophecies must be largely understood as symbolical. The coming of Christ's kingdom. The resurrection of the body. Unselfish love the key to eternal life. Judgment by the indwelling Christ. Time and eternity. The negation of evil.

CREEDS AND CREDIBILITY

I

RELIGIOUS LANGUAGE

NO theological treatise is worth reading today unless it begins by clarifying the linguistic standpoint. This is not easy to define, because the subjects of theological statements are not at first sight comparable with normal empirical facts. They are partly metaphysical, partly existential and partly aspirational. One might give as examples of each of these types (1) The existence of a personal God; (2) The experience of salvation; (3) Belief in a future life. In the body of statements which is called 'Revelation' these and similar assertions are stated as facts; and since they are not empirically justified the quality of faith is required from Christians to make them acceptable. In this sense faith is belief without empirical justification. But faith is something more than this: for its area of operation is not only intellectual. It involves commitment to a way of living based on certain non-empirical propositions. It is an act not only of intellectual assent but also of personal commitment. Yet in a sense it is empirical in action. For it is represented by Christ to be a power within the scope of the human person and capable of physical effects as well of mental dispositions. In other words Christ seems to have pointed to a power of human personality comparable with other powers such as intellection and volition which had not been previously understood or adequately utilized. He pointed man towards a dimension, not beyond human scope or understanding, which would increase his effective development. He did not give faith, but he hoped to find it, to elicit it. Faith in the irrational he never required—only in the possibility of an extension of effectiveness for good by a recognition of God as a personal over-ruling element in the human situation. He, as it were, uncovered God as a living factor in human affairs by living a life entirely based on his will, somewhat as men afterwards uncovered electricity or atomic power. Thus revelation becomes unveiling of realities instead of an arbitary divine telling of super-rational truths. Jesus lived, died and rose again by a power never before fully utilized, which his example made available to mankind. The living God is an empirical factor in the human situation, and religious language is not different from ordinary language.

It is ordinary language used so as to be inclusive of newly uncovered truths. The uncovering was so sensational both in the acts of Jesus and in their consequences that there was an immediate expression of it in such terms as the outlook of the age could achieve. These became doctrines of the new society of Christ's followers, and assent to these was required because in their ecclesiastical expression they could not be rationally comprehended. As preached, they were invested with a religious terminology some of which is becoming obsolete like the language of nineteenth-century science. Science, thinking fearlessly, abandons its obsolescent terms and statements. But Christianity is slow to do so because its statements have had saving power, and human lives are at stake. The outlines of Christian dogma are still more or less adequate expressions of truth, but, because they are obsolescent and seem irrational and have retained mythological accretions, theologians talk of religious language as if it were different from ordinary language, and of religious truth as if it were different from ordinary truth. Language is one and truth is one. There are various technical enclaves of language, and various aspects of truth. But to suggest that we must talk about religious truth in a language which is different from common speech, implies a separation of religion from 'ordinary life' which is not true. The fuller truth which is the basis of our faith requires words and expressions which are not applicable in a materialistic conception of the world. And, as it deals in the main with human hopes, aspirations and conduct in the light of the knowledge of God revealed by Christ, it is bound to speak largely in terms of moral and spiritual import. It must be mainly language about life in its psychical and non-biological aspect. But a biologist in speaking of his particular study, though he uses his own technical terms, speaks in our common language because he is trying, as we are, to express the knowledge he has gained for general understanding. Theology has developed an enormous accretion of technical terms: many are all but useless today: but those which are still alive must be explicable in such a way as to be generally understandable. They may need translation, like foreign language, but language in general must have a generally comprehensible structure, as dealing with the same facts and situations.

Analytical philosophers classify aesthetic, ethical and religious language as emotional and non-factual. Let us take an example of each. 'X is a sculptor of decadence.' Here a statement of a general kind is made. But it is made by someone. Its value is bound up with the qualifications of a particular person for judging aesthetic trends. It is made at a particular time in a particular periodical. It probably has space-time effects if only in deciding people to see or not see X's work. It originates from an aesthetic judgment of some one. But once it is made as a statement it becomes factual; its truth or falsity will be pragmatically established.

As an ethical statement one may instance 'It is wrong to steal'. This is not a mere ' "Boo" stealing' on the part of some person. It is a statement, whether true or false, about the social structure at least: it is a statement by a person concerned in the social structure in such a way as to indicate an intention to oppose theft by his influence or action. It is also historical to the extent that it implies that stealing has been found undesirable by most civilized societies. It implies that the speaker thinks he can prove its truth. As made at a particular place and time by some person of responsible intelligence, it has an empirical effect, difficult to estimate indeed, but estimable. When Moses made it there is no doubt that it considerably reduced dishonesty among the Israelites.

As a religious statement one might take, from the Creed, 'I believe in the foregiveness of sins.' This is not merely emotional. It depends on facts generally admitted as historical, and to some extent on the interpretation of these facts. As to the first ground we have the recorded teaching of Jesus, the fact of his crucifixion, which he represented and Christians received as in some sense sacrificial, and the reported prayer for his murderers on the Cross: as to the latter we have historically the general acceptance of the Cross by Christians as an atonement. Further, on the part of the person making it, it is a policy statement: he intends himself to forgive as he believes he will be forgiven. Again it is a statement about a psychological event: its maker actually feels an intense relief from the strain of remorse just as truly as if he said 'My headache is gone now.' The truth or falsity of the credal statement must no doubt be established on pragmatic lines by the subsequent actions and demeanour of the believer. But it is a factual and not an emotive statement: and any statement of fact may be false or true, even if time is required for the proof.

Now there are some religious statements which are not emotive at all: though apparently factual in form, they concern facts of which no verification is possible, or facts which appear to contradict our other verifiable knowledge. These two classes provide the real crux. As crucial cases we may cite the doctrine of the Holy Trinity, and the 'virgin birth' of Jesus Christ. They are stated as factual, but they certainly are not factual in the ordinary sense.

My contention is that they are a building up of facts into a religious structure which in itself and its purpose is non-factual but represents a life purpose and *Weltanschauung*, a symbol and means of coherence of a faith. Just as the girders, boards and concrete which form say, a railway terminal, are in themselves purely physical objects, but in this conjunction constitute a purpose of travel and a conception of how its beginning and ending should be arranged, and as the stones of a cathedral cease to have the significance of separate blocks when they are designed and built into an expression of the purpose of worship and the faith which effects its symbolic design, so innumerable facts of observation and statement from observed and human experience are built into a theological structure which conveys their conjoint explanation and conserves the purpose and conception of life which are agreed by believers to be their resultant. It is not for nothing that St. Paul uses the building as the symbol of the Church. It would be easy enough to discern a similar process in the genesis of other religions. The building could not exist without the concrete facts, the stones and other materials out of which it is constructed. But the theological building in its totality is not factual but a symbolical and purposive expression of conclusions derived from facts and the underlying realities revealed through them.

Is all this in itself an argument from analogy? Is the structure of theology in this view merely an analogy from a building? This is very far from being the case. The building has its structure, and a theology has what may be called its structure. But the analogy lies only in the fact that a theology has what may be called a structure: St. Paul found other analogies—Christians as living stones, Christ as corner stone, every part of the building depending on every other, and so on. But each analogy only deals with a partial aspect of what it illustrates. Christian conduct for example is illustrated by such analogies as keeping on straight lines, wearing the sword of the spirit, steering a true course. Theology is illustrated by similar partial analogies like 'lamb of God', 'sun of righteousness', 'the shamrock', 'leaven', the 'drag-net' and so on. But the whole is not analogical.

What is it then? All religions have what Plato would call a 'form', which is highly developed in some, and primitive in others. It is a form constructed from elements of experience and practice which are felt to have a numinous element. Some such are common to humanity: hence the similarities found in the study of comparative religion.

Apart from a scrappy and contemptuous knowledge of other

religions, the founders of Christianity had only knowledge of one supreme religious form, that of Judaism. In the time of Our Lord this religion had a form somewhat as follows: one supreme and transcendent God of righteousness, potentially Lord of all men, served by a hierarchy of angels in heaven, communicating his will to man through seers, angels, prophets and recorded events; writings believed to be inspired by him, preserved in sacred books and interpreted by scribes, set a norm of conduct which he prescribed. He was to be worshipped in one central temple and many synagogues, with prayer, sacrifices and psalmody in the temple and by prayer, reading of sacred books, and exhortation in the synagogue. He was regarded as maker of the universe, rewarder of righteousness, and punisher of sin, which comprised failure in religious practice, moral behaviour and certain ritual instructions. He intended a great destiny for his people, and would send a divine Messiah to inaugurate his reign. His worship was conducted by priests at Jerusalem, and religious instruction given by scribes and rabbis. No images were allowed. Certain great gatherings or feasts with special ceremonies were prescribed for the solidarity of Judaism. Prayer would be effective, as heard by God. The Sabbath was a sacred day: sacrifices could atone for sin. Circumcision marked the Jew as set apart. Proselytism was favoured, but there was no idea of converting the world. Gentiles were outside the pale of the 'peculiar people of God'.

Such was the religious form inherited by the first disciples of Jesus. Its features were transcendent God, moral emphasis, worship, ritual purification, prayer, sacred books, holy times and seasons, sacrifice, initiation, nationalism. The distinctively religious experiences of the Jews were co-ordinated into such a framework. Some of it had to be discarded by Christians and some new insights had to be incorporated.

The form of any religion must be more or less 'mythological': it will deal with the super-natural in symbolic language and include practices which are by purely empirical standards meaningless or useless. But 'mythological' does not mean untrue. The symbols and structure of any religion depend on a conception or form of what religion is, and in the case of Christianity the form was dominatingly provided by the noblest religion of the ancient world. The discards and accretions depended mainly on the teaching of Christ as supplemented by the religious experience of his immediate followers and the reflection of later Christians.

What was discarded from Judaism was (1) the concept of salvation by obedience to law; (2) the elimination of sins by sacrifices; (3) obligation of ritual behaviour; (4) nationalism; (5) circumcision; (6) the necessity of a central sanctuary. The inward and spiritual element in religion became far more prominent, and intellectual interpretation of religious truth gained freedom.

The general form of Jewish personal monotheism remained as the framework of 'religion' in the minds of New Testament writers, and their new experiences were bound to be expressed within it, even had this not been the tenor of the Master's teaching.[1] But there were specifically religious experiences of the Apostles and first Christians which required a modification of the Jewish form. There was firstly the experience by human beings of a Person for whom the attribute 'divine' seemed the only explanation. There were experiences of his personal presence after his crucifixion. He promised them a new divine power of holiness to inspire and direct and teach: and they experienced this power after the resurrection experience ceased. They were shattered by his crucifixion until they envisaged it as a sacrificial act of atonement and forgiveness. They recorded his teaching and found in it a new emphasis on faith, love and sincerity of spirit. And Jesus had also promised his continual presence, and appointed a special ritual which seemed to accord with the promise. He had spoken of his return, and of future judgment, which would be, perhaps, his function, and dependent

[1] The transformaton was, no doubt, initiated by Christ himself. See G. W. Lampe, *Essays on Typology*, p. 25.

on the attitude of the judged to himself. He had emphasized a hope of eternal life after death.

The form of Hebrew religion was found capable of including these new numinous experiences, but it had to be profoundly altered to make room for an immanent Godhead. The unity and transcendence of God was fundamental. It was conserved by the doctrine of the Trinity. The personality of Jesus Christ as divine was explained by the doctrine of the Incarnation, and a belief in his virgin birth and ascension supplemented the certainty of his resurrection. The divine forgiveness which he preached and his crucifixion, interpreted as an atonement, rendered sacrifice obsolete: his moral teaching transcended the old religion of law and ritual; circumcision vanished from a religion intended for all mankind.

God transcendent, holy and omnipotent remained unshaken: his worship in communities of believers kept much of the Jewish elements. Moral righteousness was demanded: a priesthood remained in modified form. The Old Testament was accepted and supplemented by what became the New: it was realized as a *praeparatio evangelica*. The similarities of form in the Old and New religions were such that for some time Christianity and Judaism were not clearly distinguished by the Gentile world. In fact the form of religion into which the Christian experiences of spiritual realities were incorporated exhibited a continuity with the form of Hebrew religion though it was considerably modified in later times by the secular influence of the form of the Roman Empire.

The needs of Christian belief and worship required many linguistic additions to the religious language of Judaism. The additions were terms and statements coined to express the new supersensible realities of which Christians had become conscious through their knowledge of Christ and his revelation. The development of religious language has however proceeded mainly on the lines of the development of scientific language. The discovery of new truths requires the adoption of new terms of expression. But there is one important difference.

The form of religion already existed in a precise system when Christ came. And the expression of the newly found truths had to be adapted to the expression of earlier aspects of truth which had already found their mythological expression and were sincerely accepted by Christians. And some of the truths, both old and new, were translations into religious terminology not of factual occurrences but of spiritual certainties. That unbelievers and followers of other religions did not, and do not, share these certainties does not turn Christian statements into a new kind of language. They are a translation of spiritual experiences and certainties of super-natural facts into an accepted religious form for the expression of a faith in worship.

2

THE LIMITATIONS OF ABSTRACT RATIONALISM

ABSTRACT thought, as its name implies, endeavours to reason in such a way that the person who is thinking and his idiosyncracies count for nothing. The content of rational thinking is governed by logical rules which are, as Kant, and Aristotle before him, tried to show, 'built into' the structure of thinking. We can think rightly only in accordance with such principles as that of contradiction and sufficient reason, and only in certain categories which are classifiable. Failure to observe them vitiates our conclusions. As Professor Ryle has pointed out, category mistakes cause much false thinking. The result is that rational thinking is universal in character. Its appeal is to the common rationality of mankind. Hence philosophers who elaborated their understanding of the basic nature of things in systems, submitted their conclusions to the general judgment of reason, and were prepared to be corrected if their reasoning were proved to be false. The dialectic of philosophy normally proceeded by thesis and antithesis, and each philosopher who aspired to produce a general system was compelled to take into account the systems of his predecessors. But the whole was only a system of thought.

Although, in their working out, the great systems of past metaphysics were severely rational in method, their character depended in the main on a fundamental personal insight or intuition of the philosopher, which had to be justified as a hypothesis by its effectiveness as a basic foundation. Thus we have Heraclitus relying on his πάντα ῥεῖ. Parmenides on 'Being is: not being is not'; Democritus on the atom; Plato on the reality of general concepts; Aristotle on form and matter; Aquinas on the 'conceptual intuition' of being; Spinoza on substance *quod in se est et per se percipitur*; Leibniz on the monad; Hegel on absolute spirit; Whitehead on process and eternal objects, and so on. Each sought and found a fundamental concept on which he based his system: but he *derived it from intuition*, though indeed each would claim that his intuition was such as to be generally acceptable and even necessary. And, more than that, he would in most cases claim that the basic intuition is presented to reason, from without, as necessary. It is that upon which reason exercises itself, and therefore fundamental. Reasoning without a genuine object degenerates into logical exercises or brain-spinning. The objective intuitions, however, may be, and have been, challenged. Parmenides refused to accept the intuition of Heraclitus as basic; materialists would refuse to accept the basic intuition of Hegel. No one but Leibniz and perhaps a mathematician or two have accepted the Monad. Being, Reality and possibly Substance are as nearly unchallengeable as any intuition can be. They are *presented* to the enquiring mind, which can have no more ultimate object.

Yet they are not presented as known. Question as to their nature arises immediately. And their nature is not presented with them. It has to be investigated by reason in any system, if this is possible. As presented, they are little more than grammatical object. Rational thought is a subject–object relation, and the *quale* of the object remains to be determined, if the object is really 'other' than the thinker. If not, a kind of solipsism is the result. The attempt to make absolute mind as the object of finite mind for a complete system broke down in Aristotle's case because he knew that the real object of finite mind was the finite substance, and there was no logical path from the complete self-sufficiency of the divine thinker, the absolute subject-object, to the human philosopher whose power of abstract thought, he considered was somehow inspired 'from without'. In Hegel's case, starting from the nature of thought itself, he managed to evolve the finite mind from the absolute mind when it 'externalized itself': but the process of doing so has not convinced philosophers, and the vast thought system culminating in absolute spirit, however logical it may be, has appeared so far removed from human experience as to be not unfairly characterized as 'right off the earth'.

It seems therefore that rational thought, as distinct from its necessary logical framework, requires an object, and must endeavour to determine the nature of that object. And this enquiry, if it is not to be merely logical and as barren as that of Parmenides, must be conducted on an empirical basis. Aquinas admits this: he is frankly an empiricist. *Sensus* must precede *intellectus*. The datum must be investigated. And success in the investigation must be attained through the consensus of other minds. This is the normal procedure of science. The verification principle establishes truth. When full verification is not possible logic may establish a necessary conclusion or point to a possibility of verification, but only from assured facts. Otherwise strong probability may be established from observed facts, as in induction, or less assuredly by analogy.

In general, therefore, rational thought is barren without an objective element which must somehow be presented to the mind, and the conclusions of the thinker must be such as would be accepted by other minds whose rational processes are identical. This is the first limitation of abstract thought. *It requires a presented object*. Even if the mind operates on the presentation as, for example, may be the case in the sense of colour, or generally in what Locke called secondary ideas, even if, as Kant thought, we only know them as worked up and categorized by the mind, there must still be some basic 'other' presented to the mind as object. Even if for Berkeley, who denied any external objects, our minds operate on ideas presented to them by the Divine Mind, the ideas have to be a datum from without. The principle that rational thought requires a presented object before it can achieve anything but an examination of its own structure holds good.

In all rational thinking, therefore, I the subject think X the object and the object is not my creation, but presented. The second limitation is also fundamental. The I who think am evacuated of individual content and characteristics and situation to become merely the locus of the thinking process. The *cogito* of Descartes has been successfully assailed because the I as an entity is assumed. It is said for example that the principle should be stated as 'A process of thinking is occurring here and now'. The I in the *cogito* is only the locus of the thinking process: and the proper conclusion is not that I as a person exist, but that a mind as a locus of thinking must exist wherever there is a subject–object process of thought. In all statements the process of such thought is co-ordinating. Two objects which the I thinks are related to one another and the maker of the relation is in practice ignored. Thus I think the United States and I think United Nations, and I relate the two objects by such a statement as 'is a member state of'. Nothing is said about the I that relates, and so it tends to be forgotten. The statement assumes that every other rational I will agree. If however I say 'The Conservatives are likely to win the next election' and other 'I's' challenge the statement as probably incorrect, the I would seem to come into the picture. I may be wrong in my statement. It is the statement, not the thinker, that is in question. The statement may be true or false. Its truth or falsity depends on the relevant facts not on any qualities of the I who asserts it. Even if it is added that 'I am known to be a bad political prophet', this only means that bad political prophecies have often emanated from one thinking being. In rational subject–object thinking the truth of any statement depends on sense experience as verified or verifiable, and correct logic; and the appeal is to an assumed universality of rational process. The thinking subject is a mere locus: in making a statement I submit it to fact and logic. It doesn't really matter who 'I' am: my personality does not come into it. 'I' may have often made false statements: but any of my statements *may* be true. And the court of appeal is not, in rational thinking, my character for veracity, but fact and logic.

It is for this reason that if 'I' elaborate a system of metaphysics my appeal is to rational thought in general. I am endeavouring to get out of my personality into a view which would be taken by divine omniscience or by a consensus of rational beings.

And thus we have a second limitation of abstract, and indeed of any rational subject–object thinking—namely that the personality of the thinker is ignored: he is a locus of a statement and nothing more. Defects in my thinking may reflect discredit on my personality as a thinker: but my thoughts and statements are public property and impersonal. That is why existentialists speak of 'escaping' into subject–object thinking: the 'I' they say 'takes refuge' in it from existential thought. But the cost of the refuge is divestment of personality.

Rational subject–object thinking is further limited, except in purely formal disciplines like mathematics and logic, by the fact that *the object may be imperfectly known*. This limitation is being progressively narrowed as the sciences advance; and the progress of human control of our material environment has thereby been accelerated. But our knowledge of such objects has to be mediated through our senses and ascertained by experiment. And the discovery of fresh qualities and potentialities in them goes on apace. Scientific knowledge is constantly developing, and although the I–it relation of thinking surrounds us with a manageable world in which we feel at home, or, at least, not lost, the mysteries behind what is known are enormous still, though in our normal lives they are disregarded as completely as the ocean bottom by passengers in a liner. If, however, the objects of our thinking are not material the case is somewhat different. Concepts such as equality may be precise and almost verifiable. Concepts such as Deity may be nebulous, or even meaningless. To attempt to bring them into a range of assurance comparable with that of scientific facts is not possible unless we can define them precisely. We can for example think about the concept 'religion', but there is not much probability that my concept of it is the same as that of a person with whom I am discussing it. Plato's belief in the eternal fixity of the forms or ideas is an illusion so far as our ability to think them is concerned, though the attempt at definition has a clarifying and inspiring value. The effort to define concepts by logic, experience or scientific fact has the double value of clarification if they are real, and elimination if they are spurious.

In general then, the objects of subject–object thinking are normally imperfectly known, and though they constitute what is called knowledge and are the material on which progress from barbarism to civilization depends, they encase us in a thought environment largely of our own making and selection, though it may well be the one most suitable for our human existence.

A further limitation of normal rational thought is not fundamental, though often disadvantageous. It is what St. Thomas Aquinas calls *debilitas rationis*. Although the 'I' is ignored in it as little more than a locus of thinking, in practice the I is very prone to false reasoning. The ideal is that pure thought should be *ex specie aeternitatis* and devoid of logical error or personal weakness. But in practice, of course, it is not. The ignorance or bias of the maker of statements is notoriously subject to error; if indeed human knowledge is so limited as Bertrand Russell supposes and human reasoning so often imperfect, we are only emerging from darkness in all our rational thinking; it works pretty well on the whole, making social stability and increasing control of the world's resources possible, but its truths are not ultimate. As persons in a space–time process we have no right to complain of this, but at the same time we must admit the fallibility of human reasoning, though not of purely rational thought adequately informed. It seems that for practical purposes the quality of the I as thinker cannot be ignored. It is tested of course by the consensus or disagreement of other thinkers, and this is, on the whole, an adequate safeguard. Kant's reliance on a rationality common to mankind was unduly optimistic. In the twentieth century there has been similarly a sad awakening from the intellectual optimism of the utilitarians.

A further aspect of subject–object or rational thinking is not a fault of its method nor of the thinker; and yet requires to be mentioned. It is the vast proliferation of knowledge with which our period is afflicted. Not only subjects but sections and sub-sections of branches of knowledge now require specialists, and any attempt at a wide synthesis is met by almost insuperable difficulties. Theses are met by well supported antitheses. The wood is obscured by the trees. The task of the προκόπτων, hopeful enough as it seemed to Panaetius, is now almost insuperable. Not only is the body of facts in any field overwhelming: they are re-sorted and re-used by successive writers, and we have, as Professor T. B. L. Webster reminded the Classical Association in 1960, now to deal with books about books about books. From the aspect of scholarship this is becoming frightening: the accumulation of theses and petty researches and tabulations is only equalled by the accumulations of files in business offices. The amount of information now potentially available on any subject is so vast that it is no wonder that computers have been called in to deal with it, and that serious research has to be done by teams. The human ant-like accumulation of information, resulting in great heaps all over the arid landscape, as in S. Africa, is daunting for those who share Heraclitus' aspiration for 'accurate steering for a balanced life'. The clarity of wide, general and authoritative guidance is essential. And yet today, as in the time of the sceptical Academy, παντὶ λόγῳ λόγος ἀντικεῖται, seems horribly true. Every critic can marshal a formidable array of facts against every attempt to be conclusive. All but the minutest scholarship is haunted by the thought of how much more ought to have been known and investigated.

So it appears that the existentialist taunt that we are escaping from realities when we seek safety in comfortable 'problematic' areas of subject–object thinking needs qualification. It is more like getting out of the frying pan into the fire, if our escape is into such a dazing multiplicity of facts and statements and theories and hypotheses. Modern man is in danger of being choked and stifled by his accumulations of knowledge, and attempts to make decisions after weighing all relevant information are almost sure to fail except in very narrow fields.

Accordingly we now turn to consider the suggested alternative, namely existential thought.

3

THE LIMITATIONS OF EXISTENTIAL THOUGHT

EXISTENTIAL thinking claims to have a deeper relevance to the human situation than rational thought of the subject-object type. It begins from inside human existence and asks what are the reactions of the personal existent to the situation in which he finds himself—namely 'being in the world'. The ego exists in a stream of otherness which he fails to understand: it does not know how it began to be there but it has certain intuitive assurances, namely that it will assuredly cease to exist in it at some undetermined point of time, and that meanwhile it has freedom to make decisions, and that these must be made. The necessity of making them while involved in the unknown, and the realization that they will have consequences which it cannot predict, produces an insight of 'care' or anxiety which is an inevitable accompaniment of existence. The consciousness of freedom and responsibility, without adequate grounds on which they can be exercised rightly, is bad enough, but when this is accompanied by the certainty of death, and the ignorance of what may follow it, if anything does, provides another existential category—despair. It is mitigated in the case of a Christian existentialist by a numinous feeling of the reality of God, supporting our frailty and transience, and this for him results in the insight of 'presence'. Presence leads the Christian existentialist to a further insight: the divine presence demands 'fidelity', and fidelity extends itself to inter-human relations as well. The atheist, being without these supports, sometimes finds the whole affair of living 'ludicrous', or if frustrated at all points in his efforts to find a firm footing, *viscous*. These insights are asserted as being fundamental to the human situation, and deeper than psychological feelings. They are part of the reality which we have to face, not more malaises curable by psychotherapy.

The human situation is indeed one of much difficulty: for though each of us has a project of himself as he knows he could be—his essence, the project, according to Sartre, is always in front of us, and unrealizable because of frustrations: actually existence precedes essence.

Existence, however, to Heidegger is possibility. Man is both subject and object to himself, and so must think of himself differently from his normal thought of objects. His being is never complete, always a possibility. By recognizing the transitoriness and insecurity of his actual situation he may choose authentic existence, or he may prefer to immerse himself as a physical creature in a world of physical objects, and construct an inauthentic existence in which he makes himself comfortable until realities force themselves upon him. He may in this existence have theoretical understanding of his surroundings, such as all forms of science provide: but to face the facts of existential self-understanding, in spite of the care and anxiety which they bring, is of far greater importance. Such understanding is reached by phenomenological examination of existential experiences. Fear, for example, is a realization of the world as that from which something terrible may appear and reveal to the *Dasein* (existent being) his possibility of danger: he is in a world in which his being is threatened. Fear is a way-of-being of the *Dasein*. Or again the existential concept of fallenness, in which the authentic self has been abandoned to the world, includes temptation, by which man wants to surrender to his inauthentic being, contentment, illusory but comforting because man feels at home in his world, and alienation, because he has cut himself off from his true self.

Existential thinking brings its content into a deeper personal relevance than rational thought. Conscience, for example, has been treated in various ways, theological, social, psychological and philosophical; to Heidegger, conscience discloses man to himself. It is a recall to authentic existence from the fallen state of immersion in the world of things. It is the call of the authentic self to the fallen self, and belongs to the existential self in its aspect of possibility. The authentic self remains a possibility, and conscience recalls it to the man who has allowed himself to become unauthentic, in moments of disclosure, induced perhaps by anxiety or impotence or discontent. Or again, let us take history. The existential understanding of history is that which has its origin in the past as what has happened to man, but affects his present. It is man's way of being as historical: it affects his existence now, presenting possibilities of authentic existence as repeatable. If history belongs to man, and man is in his being different from nature, the findings of the historian must be relevant to human nature, that is to man as possibility. They disclose past events as present possibilities. Those theologians, like Bultmann, who think existentially, have naturally made much of this view in decrying the 'facticity' of salvation-events, and enhancing their urgency as present proclamation of God's mercy.

The value of existential thinking would appear to be mainly religious because it recalls man from 'the world' to his real situation as existent. Without God, he is adrift in an uncomprehended process. With God he can pass into authentic existence. He meets both God and 'other people' on an I–Thou level. We are 'concerned' with others as persons, not as instruments, when we truly meet them: our existential meeting with the living Christ is said to bring deliverance from the wrath of the Living God, which is what is due to our sin. The kerygma of God, made through Christ, offers a return to full authentic existence from the preoccupations of this-worldly 'concern' in which we try to escape from our true selves.

Without this religious interpretation it would appear that existentialism has little to offer to man except a possible full acceptance of his mortality and frustrations, and a life 'condemned to be free'. In this we accept ourselves as being what we are in the eyes of other people, as frustrated by them in any effort to realize our project of ourselves. We make our own decisions, with a sense of legislating for all mankind in doing so, and without the least expectation that mankind will be affected by our legislation or choices.

Except in the field of religion, and perhaps even there as well, the limitations of existential thinking are narrowly drawn. An intuitive awareness of our human situation, derived from introspection, will condition a more genuine approach to life, but has nothing to guide us for living in the world, which is our necessary state and for which normal rational thinking is our instrument. When we start solely from ourselves in contemplating the great universe and God, we shall not get very far. A Christian existentialist might perform all his actions in an aura of love for mankind, but that would not greatly help him in deciding what actions were needed and what ill-conceived and useless. The existentialist is irretrievably self-centred, and even if, as a Christian, he surrenders himself as inauthentic, there is nothing except feeling to guide him in so-called authentic existence. In fact Karl Barth's doctrine of the Word of God is the true complement of Bultmann's existentialist Christianity because according to it, authentic guidance is continually given from the transcendent deity, by his Word. Existential thinking has no value whatever in the normal decisions of 'inauthentic existence' in the world. As everyone willy-nilly has to be here, and to act here, rational thought and particularly science will be inseparable necessities. And however the existentialist may decry the value of a mundane involvement, he will have to exist and think in it for most of the time. In fact his existentialism will only provide an attitude towards living in the world, and a deeper realization of what it means or does not mean. The field of such thought, though important in its depth, is too narrow in its scope. The attempt to live and think existentially all the time would produce a temperament of morbidity or religious mania, and in the extremes, a suicidal tendency arising from loneliness and introspective despair. Its restless quest for meaning of a non-rational kind has produced a spate of incoherent insights, and considerable literary brilliance, but no systematic philosophy and little agreement, except in general attitude, among those who profess it.

Existentialist thinkers strictly should have confined themselves to expressions of the human situation in terms of insights relying for their effect on the instinctive agreement of others who experience similar reactions. An example of this might be the amused assent often given to Sartre's remark that 'Hell is other people'. Their proper medium of expression, which has been widely used, lies in plays and novels which win assent by a kind of sympathy. But not all existentialists have so limited themselves. They have tried to use their vital insights as concepts, which they are not, and reasoned about them in a way perilously close to their despised subject–object thinking. Vital and emotional processes like 'understanding', 'fearing', 'being anxious', feeling free, or feeling lost, or feeling 'thrown' cannot be hypostatized or conceptualized, they can only be experienced. To turn them into concepts and try for example to understand understanding leads to an infinite regress.

The idea that subject–object thinking leads to unreal mental and institutional constructions which serve only as escapes from the existential situation, and make man falsely 'at home' in the world has a certain religious truth. Professor John McQuarrie has shown that it has close affinities with the thought of St. Paul and St. John in the New Testament. In these writers 'somatic' existence in the flesh is unreal in contrast with life in the spirit, and the believer has reached authentic existence 'in Christ'. He is 'not of this world' if he is truly 'in Christ'. But when the spiritual doctrine came to be worked into human society, as it had to be if it were to be effective for human salvation, the Church had to be bound together by intellectual unity of belief, by corporate unity of organization, by moral unity of ethics, and by formality in worship. The city of God had to find expression in human society, to which at this stage it inevitably belongs. All this is far more than escapism from our true existential situation. The latter always underlies, more or less, the Church's formal expression, and inspires its spiritual life: but, without the 'outward and visible' expression, the inward and spiritual grace would evaporate. This is even more true of society in general: human nature is as much social as individual. Progress in social coherence and mutual help has always depended on rational thought and organization as much as upon a sense of reality in I–Thou relationships.

4

THE LIMITATIONS OF PRESENT THEOLOGICAL THINKING

ORTHODOX theology has been shaken by assaults from many directions in the twentieth century. The existentialist attack has been indicated in the last chapter. Its gravamen lies in the decrial of rational subject–object thinking as evasive of man's true situation. Theology begins by making God an object of our thought, which, it is asserted, the transcendent deity can never be to his creatures. God as hitherto conceived by theologians is said to be 'dead'. He does not exist anywhere in or outside the universe: he is only realizable 'in depth', and as a supreme reality of love exemplified in Jesus as 'the man for others'. Consequently theological statements about his nature, such as Trinitarian and Christological doctrines provided, are said to be quite inadequate, and factual statements as to his historical actions are of a mythological type. Behind such criticism of orthodox theology there lies a truth of transcendence which must accompany, and always has accompanied, human efforts to conceive God. And although the theology of Karl Barth is not existential, it supplements the existential insights by providing what they cannot provide, a theology. Barth knows intellectually two things only about God, namely that he is our Creator and that he speaks. From the word of God as spoken through Christ and the Bible we learn a great deal more about him. Our task is not to reason about this, but to obey. Barth accepts the articles of the Apostles' Creed, in his own sense, because as he says they are founded on the 'word written': but the Bible as such is accepted almost uncritically as our only foundation document. So in theology it is a case of 'ours not to reason why, ours but to do and die', trusting in the divine kerygma, as set forth in the

Book. This uncritical acceptance of revealed truth lends itself to a powerful Calvinism, and to an interpretation of salvation as *sola fide* which finds its main support in the Pauline writings.

In fact, paradox is asserted as fundamental to theological thought, as for example by Niebuhr. Paradoxes admit of no rational solutions. Philosophical theology is discounted: so is comparative religion: the general schema, so far as it goes, is consistent; but only so far as it goes. The demands upon faith are overwhelming. Barth will have nothing to do with existential demythologizing. The existentialist has recourse to the meaning of past history for present existents. For Barth the present existent has only one function, to hear the word and to obey. Faith is the gift of God to him, grace is the sole ground of the salvation realized by faith. The great stumbling block to those who cannot accept Barth's interpretation is how the Word can be known to be the Word. The narratives of the Birth of Christ, for example, have inevitably provoked questions of authenticity: to Barth (*Credo*, p. 70) it speaks of a creation taking place in Mary, a mystery preserved by the Christology of the early church. Those who doubt it are limiting the theology of 'free grace': it should be left uncriticized.

Barth would regard the Word as self-authenticating. But can he also say that the means by which the Word is communicated are also self-authenticating? The preacher may proclaim as God's word a doctrine of an ethical kind, such as sabbatarianism which is by no means established in the New Testament. The only test of the authenticity of his message will be by rational criticism. Christ often taught by vivid paradox or exaggeration. Are we not to dare to understand this? Passages in the New Testament have been shown by valid scholarship to be of doubtful origin: do they communicate the word, or not? Homo sapiens, forbidden to exercise his reason except in ordered presentation of what is revealed, and compelled to obey against his own integrity of judgment, is in a state of intellectual slavery for which his mind cannot have been intended. Barthianism itself is only one interpretation. Are those who cannot accept it damned?

Of all modern systems of theological thinking Barth's is the most limited. In effect it denies our right to think theologically at all.

When we turn to Bultmann we meet one who has probed the extremes of criticism without losing his faith. He finds it from the very existential mode which has made Heidegger atheist. For the authentic existence which Heidegger supposes to be attainable by facing the situation of being in a world alien to the self, free for decision, but doomed to annihilation sooner or later, has a much more satisfactory character for the Christian. Inauthentic being now becomes losing oneself in the world, regarding oneself as belonging to it with a consequent endeavour to make it one's home. The world is a constant threat to authentic existence which is not of this world, a spiritual rather than a somatic way of being. Man-in-the-world is estranged from his true self: his freedom is his possibility of decision for a life in the spirit. Professor John McQuarrie[1] rightly finds in Bultmann's theology a deep relevance to personal religion. It is remarkable how closely existential concepts correspond to Pauline theology. The kerygma awakens man by God's word to an authentic self-understanding. Faith is the answer to its call for decision; the self-analysis of the existentialist gives an ontological foundation to the spiritual call for conversion and the 'given' and spirit-guided life. But McQuarrie rightly, as it seems, finds deficiencies in Bultmann's version of Christianity. Theology for Bultmann is the analysis of human existence on the understanding given by faith. But this would appear to give an existential theology 'detached from any religious basis in the activity of God'. Statements of his mighty acts are historical and not existential: but Bultmann is driven to radical demythologizing by his existentialism. Further, his doctrine of the Holy Spirit fails to be fully personal and transcendent.

[1] *An Existentialist Theology*.

'Theology cannot rest in existential statements but must go on to speak of God and the transcendent'. Further as one might expect the doctrine of the Church receives very scant attention.

One might well expect this, and it points to a fundamental defect in the existential approach. It takes the part for the whole. Deeply as it illuminates the personal aspect of religion, its preoccupation with the individual existent and his situation virtually excludes the spiritual aspect of man as a social being, and, even worse than this, the transcendent reality of God is merely a background condition of our existence, and such revelation as he has given of himself is ignored. The treatment of this by theologians is decried as merely subject–object thinking: but if we are to *think* about God at all apart from feeling him, we must think of him as object. To make God an object of thought no more diminishes his majesty than to make love an object of thought diminishes the greatness of love. The limitation of Bultmann's brilliant insights is imposed by their sole dependence on the point of view of the human existent. The scope of thought cannot be so circumscribed, nor can intellectual thought be so depreciated.

The critique of theology by logical analysis has had one salutary effect in compelling Christians to ask what they really mean, and to clarify their statements. The gravamen of the attack derived from the charge of meaninglessness. Theological propositions are often such as cannot be verifiable; to assert that they are based on revelation or matters of faith leaves scientific and logical thinkers coldly sceptical. Their question as to what would 'count against them' seems to be met with evasions. On the assumption of the existence of God as the supreme personal Being some of them can be justified: but his existence cannot be rationally proved. To reply that he transcends reason, or to assert the simultaneous truth of paradoxes which violate the principles of identity or sufficient reason, could well appear to be evasive.

There have been several recent attempts to digest or parry

the attack of Analysis on theological statements, and to show that they can still be meaningful.

Professor R. B. Braithwaite[1] suggests that the use of religious assertions is linked with that of moral assertions, and indicates intention to behave in a certain way. The intention to behave in religious assertions expresses what is called religious conviction. The difference between religious and moral statements is that the former refer to a story as well as to an intention. The story need not be true empirically, but it defines or prescribes a line of action. Thus a religious belief in eternal life, based on the story of the resurrection, indicates an intention to live in the assumption that this life is not all, and that we are destined for a life of higher quality hereafter.

The weaknesses of this theory are fairly obvious. In the first place, not all religious assertions have a moral character, nor do they all indicate a policy of behaviour. As a simple example Ps. 65.12 reads 'Thou crownest the year with thy goodness: thy paths drop fatness'. It expresses, metaphorically indeed, a conviction that the bounty of harvest is the gift of the lord of nature, and is an act of praise, not of intention to do anything about it. Neither has it any moral import. The sphere of morality, as understood in the West, is consequential for the most part on the beliefs of the Christian religion: each religion has moral consequences to a greater or less degree for its adherents: Christianity in particular has strong moral and social implications: but in its demands it often transcends the purely ethical, and in its worship it passes right out of the mundane condition of good and evil. Truth, beauty and holiness are absolute qualities which have no positive opposites. Falsity, ugliness and 'profanity' are merely terms indicating their absence.

A more serious weakness in Professor Braithwaite's position has often been pointed out, namely that it would appear that the truth of the story on which the behaviour policy is based in religious assertions, may be irrelevant. For example, in

[1] *An Empiricist's View of Christian Belief*, CUP, 1955.

Hinduism we find a Rigvedic hymn telling of the origin of the four castes in Purusha, the original man.

> The Brahman was his mouth, of both his arms was the Rajanya made,
> His thighs became the Vaisya, from his feet the Sundra was produced.[1]

This story, entertained by religious assertion, involves the intention or policy of the caste-system; and why not, if the truth of the story does not matter? Any religious myths may be on a par with Christian myths. And a decision between these would only be made by their moral and social effects. We are back at the 'salutory stories' by which Plato would indoctrinate his youthful citizens, if we are to make any choice.

The truth of a story may indeed be irrelevant to the policy and intention implied by it. The story of the Good Samaritan associated with the religious assertion that it is good, or it is God's will, that we should befriend our neighbour in adversity, need not be true factually and will have purely moral import apart from the belief of the Christian that it was told by Christ. But if it be taken as a fact that it was really told by divine authority it gains an added force as being more than merely ethical. There is much more in religious assertions than an intention to act in a certain way as suggested by the accompanying story.

R. M. Hare[2] is prepared to agree that religious or theological statements can no longer be accepted as providing factual information about man and the universe. He prefers to regard them as statements of a personal attitude (he calls it a 'blik') on which the assertor takes his stand. He commits himself, in adopting this attitude, to see the world in a certain way and act accordingly; thus his faith statements have meaning, even if they are meaningless if taken as statements about 'how things are'. Presumably Hare would admit that the Christian 'blik' provides better results than would, for example, a solipsist 'blik'. There are obviously good 'bliks' and bad 'bliks': but how to distinguish them? Results of 'bliks' are so varied that

[1] D. W. Gundry, *Religions*, Macmillan, 1958, p. 86.
[2] R. M. Hare, *New Essays*.

they can scarcely be made the criterion or indeed assessed. The only test would appear to be that of truth to facts or realities of some kind. A lunatic's 'blik', e.g. that he is made of glass, could be distinguished from a sane man's by empirical means. But when the 'bliks' are mythical the distinction between a true and a false myth is hard to make. The early Christians when faced with Gnostic 'bliks' appealed to historical fact: and this has hitherto been the orthodox Christian reaction.

In fairness, however, to Braithwaite, Hare and others it must be remembered that what they are doing is not so much a decrial of orthodox beliefs as an attempt to counter the negative effects of analytical philosophy by showing that, even on its axioms, there are senses in which the faith of Christians is meaningful in spite of them. To formulate a logically respectable Christianity appears to them necessary in face of the modern outlook. Bonhoeffer tried to meet it by a secular Christianity but did not live to develop his answer. His suggestions, however, have stimulated thought so urgently that Christians of today cannot ignore them.

We have already considered the existentialist answer. Bultmann, in effect, tries to reduce all theological statements about God to statements about the human existential situation, 'exhaustively and without remainder'. But as van Buren has shown, Bultmann is inconsistent because he adds that authentic existence has only become possible for man 'because of Jesus of Nazareth'. If the historical fact of Jesus is necessary before man can achieve authentic existence there must be some eternal significance in his life and death. Bultmann explains this by calling the Cross an 'eschatological event'. The past event lives in its present proclamation, because history is only alive in individual experience. Plausible though this may sound, it is not the New Testament understanding of the Cross and Resurrection, and it ties Christian Faith to a philosophy which is by no means generally accepted. An eternal event is a contradiction in terms: an event with eternal significance is a different thing.

The pursuit of this line of thought has, in fact, led S. M. Ogden[1] to dispense with any saving act in any 'incarnation'. The claim that God is revealed in Jesus only means that the God, who is to be found everywhere and in all religions to some extent, is 'decisively manifested' in Jesus. As van Buren pertinently asks, why 'decisively'? There seems to be no adequate reason.

There remain to be considered two other attempts to reply to the analytical 'organon'. Professor I. T. Ramsey[2] following Ryle and others, notes that our statements are constantly made in different categories of thought, and that for example when we say 'This tree is dying' and 'the sunset is dying' and 'I am dying to go to Greece' we are not speaking in the same categories. The categorical status of religious beliefs involves, as he says, a discernment followed by a commitment. When we use religious language we are playing a different language game from, say, when we make a scientific statement. For the religious man God is a key-word, an ultimate explanation expressive of the kind of commitment he professes: its use is similar to the ultimate explanation of a free choice, which is 'because I am I'. In making a religious statement we are using a particular logical language game indicated by one word used as a model and another as a qualifier. The model suggests the type which we have in mind, and the qualifier indicates that there is something unusual in the statement. So when we call God our heavenly Father, we indicate by the model Father certain qualities of Fatherhood as attributable to him, and by the qualifier 'heavenly' that his fatherhood is not the same as ours. The qualifier plus model bring about a discernment situation plus a commitment to God's fatherhood. Again when we say he ascended into Heaven, the model 'ascended' and the qualifier 'into Heaven' bring a discernment that we are speaking of something more than a fact, and a commitment to Christ's eternal reign. 'The empirical basis of Christian

[1] *Christ without Myth*, Harper & Row, New York.

[2] *Religious Language*, SCM Press, 1957. (He is now Bishop of Durham.)

doctrine', Ramsey says, 'is always to be sought in such distinctive and unique disclosure situations'. A special type of logical impropriety is needed to express the Christian message, to bring about the 'dropping of the penny', the disclosure on which the commitment depends. However, as Ramsey admits, 'Christian doctrine will never give us a blue-print of God. It will talk of God as best it can, but never in terms of more than models, metaphors, key-ideas and the rest'. Its language is 'likely to bristle with improprieties'. Theological statements generally are made in a context of worship which involves both discernment and commitment, and must accordingly show an odd logical structure.

Ramsey's answer therefore to the charge of meaninglessness is, briefly, to say that on purely empirical lines theological statements are meaningless: but that their phrasing, in its oddness, indicates a discernment to the believer which is more than factual, and involves for him a commitment of faith. It is a particular 'language game' which is full of meaning for the Christian once the qualifier illuminates the model as a model and the discernment occurs. Religious language is thus defended from the charge of being illogical: but it is difficult to see what more has been done. The question whether the discernment is true or merely a 'blik' remains unanswered. The 'disclosure situation' when realized may bring an overwhelming sense of truth, but why? The only answer is a kind of logical 'stop-word' like 'I am I'—namely 'because it is true'.

Finally Paul van Buren[1] has attempted to divest the Gospel and Christian Theology of any expression, including even the very name of God, which cannot have any clear logical meaning to an empiricist. The result is a purely human Jesus, who lived a life of complete freedom for the service of mankind and died on the Cross. The accounts of this life are written in the light of the Resurrection and the consequent recognition of Jesus as 'Lord'. What then was the Resurrec-

[1] *The Secular Meaning of the Gospel*, SCM Press, 1963.

tion? It was certainly not resuscitation, which, as a mere event, could not produce faith. The term indicates a sudden realization on the part of his followers that the perfect freedom in which Jesus lived was contagious. He 'appeared' to them in a new light as the one who could liberate all lives. They looked back on his life and death with new eyes. They 'gained a new perspective on life and history'. 'The confession "Jesus is Lord", ascribing universality to a particular man, constituted a certain understanding of self, man, history, and the whole world', and had Jesus as its norm. The 'appearances', on realization of the contagious freedom given by Jesus, created a situation of discernment with an accompanying commitment to his way of life. This new discernment is expressed in the languages of revelation, Easter, 'the illumination of the Holy Spirit' and conversion. Because the sources for the history of Jesus present him as fulfilling in his person the destiny of his people, his history receives illumination from that of the people from whom he came. The fact that at Easter the disciples came to see Jesus in a new way implies that they had seen him in an old way, and therefore Easter faith depended on their memory of Jesus. Thus Christianity may be called a historical religion though it originates in a discernment. Apart from Jesus there are only false conceptions of God: he is the man who was free for others, and his freedom was realized as contagious. Since his life was lived for man, his death which was its consequence 'was spoken of as a death for us'. In fine 'The meaning of the Gospel is its use on the lips of those who proclaim it. The Christian has seen a man of remarkable and particular freedom, and this freedom has become contagious for him as it was for the apostles at Easter. So his history and Easter have produced a situation of discernment, reorienting the Christian's perspective on the world'. Statements of faith express and commend a particular way of seeing the world, and an appropriate way of life. And the norm of the Christian perspective is the account of Jesus of Nazareth in the New Testament documents.

Thus van Buren endeavours to satisfy the 'secular' thinker who sees no use or meaning in the word God. But the New Testament documents make it abundantly clear that Jesus himself did not agree with him, and attributed all that he was and did to God, whom he called his 'Father'. The Resurrection has further been evacuated of any meaning. Apart from the gospel narratives of the appearances and the empty tomb, which have been discredited by some modern critics, St. Paul's statement[1] that Jesus was seen by Peter, by the twelve, by five hundred brethren, by James and by all the apostles, can scarcely be watered down to mean that Peter and the others after the death of Jesus came to realize that the freedom with which Jesus had lived was contagious and had become their own. 'If Christ be not raised from the dead,' St. Paul says, 'then is our preaching vain, and your faith also is vain.' This not the expression of a mere discernment of the human life of Jesus in a new light, as infectiously liberative.

To make the language of Christian faith conform to the supposed demands of logicians and of the 'modern mind', van Buren is prepared to sacrifice the whole area of worship, and leave only an ideal of unselfish and philanthropic human living based on an 'infectious' human example. The liberation effected by this discernment of what Jesus really was, seems to include a throwing aside of the past of a human life with its sins and failures, and a renewal inspired by one who differed from Socrates in his liberating power only in degree. If there is no God, presumably there is no ultimate justice, no deliverance from past sins, and no hope of an eternal life. These have hitherto been the mainstays of Christian faith, and they are not lightly to be exchanged for a realization that self-giving love is the secret of true living. If the resurrection is merely what van Buren thinks it was, does it only consist for us in realizing from the kerygma, when we hear it, that Jesus is the way, the truth and the life. We have that realization already, and much more, in orthodoxy.

[1] 1 Cor. 15. 5–7.

With considerable ingenuity, van Buren tries to show that traditional Christology still has a meaning compatible with his interpretation of Jesus. The doctrine of the two natures of Christ is a way of stating that the human history of Jesus is different from the discernment of his life to be unique and his freedom contagious. The stories connected with his birth cannot be factual, they are expressions of awe and thanksgiving for the coming of such a man into the world. The doctrine of the Holy Spirit expresses the Christian's sense of being 'grasped' by the 'norm' of the life of Jesus. In speaking of him as sinless we are acknowledging that his life is our 'norm'. The confession of him as Son of God says only that the Christian's freedom derives from his freedom. The two great commandments to love God and to love our neighbour 'can only mean that we are to love our neighbour on the model of Jesus in his freedom.'

There is much more of this type of exposition: its net result is to evacuate religion of the transcendent, at the bidding of modern secular thought. But religion hitherto has always been thought to deal primarily with the transcendent which has been believed to be the basis and rationale of human agapeistic behaviour. It is not to be lightly cast aside at the bidding of logical consistency and godless humanism, however nobly the life of Jesus is conceived.

5

THE LIMITATIONS OF MYSTICISM

WE have seen that abstract thought requires a conceptual object, that existential thought has only a kind of intersubjective validity, and that religious thinkers have either denied the ability of our thinking to comprehend the ways of God, or sought to reduce Christianity from the status of universal truth to a discernment of a way of life which evades the logicians because it is expressed in a peculiar language pattern, explained as valid for faith alone.

Almost every religious person has experiences which seem to transcend normal processes of thought whether rational or existential. There seems to be within our reach an area of spiritual apprehension which can only be attained when there is some elimination of the personal subject. It is as though we lose our anchorage on earth and drift on a spiritual tide of illumination which brings with it a sense of supreme happiness and liberation. The cost of this spiritual detachment is great, but so is the reward. It involves an ascetic control of bodily needs, a discarding of worldly ambitions and entanglements, and a life of prayer and meditation. It is described as an approach of the alone to the Alone, transcending intellectual thought, and even the personality of the mystic. He is as it were caught up into an experience of transcendence, and taken out of himself and into a greater reality. The 'vision of God' may or may not be vouchsafed, but, if it is, there is a sense of inexpressible holiness and joy. The mystic receives an inspiration which seems to transform his life, but no explicit revelation of God. The reality of his vision seems to him so overwhelming as to make our transitory life unreal, but his return to it is as from a far country of which little can be told, and yet, it seems, of infinite worth. There can be little doubt that it is a real experience of God, and that the divine and ineffable is 'there' to be experienced, and yet somehow the mystical path seems to be outside the pattern of normal living, and to involve so complete a transcendence of normal personality that it is certainly not for everyman, but only for a spiritual élite.

It must be possible to know God, to love and to obey him, within the possibilities which are open to every man, his reason, his moral sense, and his loves. To divest oneself of these while still living a human life, may bring one into a spiritual area with which some contact is possible even here and now. It may well purify earth-bound mortality, but it will give no chart of the unbounded seas, and no intellectually communicable certainties. Mysticism will bind together all religions, since all religions have had their mystics, but it will not establish religious truth. There is an element of awe, wonder and glory in all religion, and mystical experience assures us of its reality. But since it is in essence super-human and super-rational and super-existential it is no answer to the general need of the knowledge of God, or to the problem of presenting it to an unbelieving world. Mysticism can give a purification of the soul, and a certainty of spiritual realities, but it cannot answer questions as to its content or its validity: it can easily be confused and contaminated by baser 'hunches' of spiritual insight, and only authenticates itself to those who have had genuine experiences, after paying the price. 'Testing the spirits whether they be of God' was a difficult problem even in the early church, and St. John's solution, 'Every spirit that confesseth not that Jesus Christ is come in the flesh is not of God', is only rough and ready, and does not cover many cases of spiritual and mystical claims.

Besides, mysticism is by no means confined to Christianity. It is really, as it was to Plotinus, a post-philosophical rather than a post-religious exercise. What the mystic transcends in his vision is the intellectual sphere in particular, as the least individual aspect of his human personality. The area of emotion and sense has been left far behind when he enters on meditation, the practice of pure thought. The illumination, if it comes, is post-subjective and unanalysable. It is an intimation of a reality 'beyond', but in no way assists our understanding of it, still less its formulation as religious belief.

6

THE LIMITATIONS OF SCIENTIFIC THOUGHT

UP to this point we have found limitations in most of the principal modes of human thinking, except that which has become dominant and apparently successful in our own day, namely empirical scientific investigation. Reliance here rests upon sense experience as extended by instruments and verified by observation and experiment. The scientist isolates a specific area, and studies it intensively: his method is, however, similar in all areas of research. It is severely factual in observation: results are classified: general conclusions, wide or narrow, are formed, and hypotheses are tested by experiment. If they seem probable, they are brought into a wider context of similar fields of study for a test of coherence. And results thus obtained are used practically, or held theoretically with a certain reserve, and not as absolute findings. Wider scientific generalizations are often formulated but confidence in them is held with a caution, namely that future discoveries may make them obsolete. In the purely formal sciences, mathematics and logic, results seem to be assured, but they are devoid of practical content until they are applied to objects of a physical kind. In certain aspects of physical science, like astronomy and nuclear physics, the investigations and conclusions pass into an area in which it is difficult to say where observation ends and pure mathematics takes over and 'whatness' becomes a matter of behaviour patterns. Observation, experiment and deduction from them are paramount; but knowledge of how things behave and happen is continually increasing, and of course is leading, with incredible swiftness, towards human control of the physical entourage of the human mind. No one can tell how far this process is likely to go. It is already eliminating from the popular mind many conceptions of a spiritual kind. Theology has received shocks in so far as it included cosmology in its purview. Psychology has modified former conceptions of sin, and religious fears or obsessions. Sociology has had a powerful effect on traditional Christian morality. Faith in medicine and surgery has affected conceptions of faith in divine intervention and prayer. Fatalism or chance have encroached on belief in Providence, and conceptions of Heaven and Hell have lost their vividness and reality for most people. The scientific revolution has brought, generally, such sweeping alterations of religious conceptions that they cannot be convincingly presented in their old forms to educated people of today. That is, of course, in so far as the religious conceptions have been based on physical facts.

Yet, for all its triumphs, science cannot answer questions which are of fundamental importance: in some cases it can give answers, but they are unsatisfying. It can say that, so far as physical evidence goes, there is little or nothing to justify belief in a future life. It can base ethics on social evolution and common sense, but it cannot explain the compulsive aspect of the moral sense. It can show the non-existence of God as a feature of the physical universe, but cannot banish him from human thought and instinct. It can explain, generally, what happens on physical lines, but cannot prove the non-existence of spiritual causes. It can describe vital and psychological processes, but is silent on the mystery of personality. Science can analyse the brain, and imitate its action by computers, but cannot say whether the brain is in itself originative or instrumental. It can map out the universe, but cannot account for man's awe and wonder in regarding it. It is silent on the mysteries of creative imagination—art, music, poetry, worship, are largely outside its sphere. And the central mystery of love can only be touched on its lower fringe by biology and sociology.

In fine, between physical facts and human values, there seems to be no road. Whether there is a road between human values and divine realities remains to be seen. Human beings certainly value the increasing benefits made available by science with wide concern. But they value them not as facts but as instruments for their physical welfare and scope of activity. The range of our movement, our sight and our hearing have been enormously extended by machines and instruments. So have our prospects of food and health. But the capacity for enjoyment of these benefits has not increased, and the use made of them still depends on qualities of character and taste, apart from the satisfactions derived solely by our physical organism. A feeling of well-being and of health and of the wider scope provided by wealth are certainly deeply valued; a self-centred materialist might well regard them as the only real values. But if all others were of the same opinion, envy, violence, despondency and satiety would quickly bring his little paradise to an end. The uses and abuses of their new resources by human beings seem to increase in proportion to their acquisition.

And yet, as by a primal urge, the drive for ever new scientific progress continues apace, without reflection as to whether it will be conducive to human happiness or well-being. Millions are poured into space research without, apparently, much purpose except that of rivalry, without much assurance of benefits to be derived from it, and in spite of the waste of resources which could confer certain benefits on mankind. There is a kind of commitment of humanity to further and further probing of the physical universe without any definite object, hope or control. There is a faith that more and more knowledge is desirable, and an immense excitement in exploring the unknown; but scientific thought is without any ultimate object; it takes no account of ultimate values; and accepts the dictation of empirical facts. The price paid by technological man for the control of his environment is the atrophy of other faculties of the mind apart from the senses, which bind him to the physical world; he becomes increasingly mechanical in his work and sensual in his behaviour when work is intermitted, though his sensuality may be only expressed in terms of rest, escapism or brief excitements.[1] His thinking on general matters tends to be fed in from newspapers and radio, and his field of expert knowledge is narrow and specialist. There are indeed many scientists whose field is wide and who are able to extend their interests and speak authoritatively on topics of general importance. There are also those who leave the empirical disciplines for a time and digress into philosophy or theology. But such excursions are not scientific in character; the limitations of strictly empirical thinking remain: it is confined to facts experienced through the senses, verifiable by experiment, and unable to convey any truths or values which are not of a physical or mathematical or experiential type.

[1] See E. R. G. Mure, *Retreat from Truth*.

7

THE PERSONAL ELEMENT IN THINKING

THE framework of normal human thinking is rational. But rationality is a regulative principal of a complex whole, and reason alone does not normally supply the content. Of course when our thought is occupied by an algebraic or geometrical proposition its content is susceptible of purely rational treatment. In dealing with accounts also the subject matter is largely symbolic and regulated by mathematical laws. The person thinking in such cases is not involved, and is virtually mechanical: in fact his place can increasingly be taken by a computer.

The involvement of the personal thinker with the subject of his thought is much more complex. In scientific thinking the conclusions are mainly based on the behaviour of the empirical subject matter, but another element has entered in, namely the desire to know. This desire is also an incentive in philosophical thinking, attracted by the unknown, and accompanied by the hope of attainment. In theology the *amor intellectualis Dei* is a major incentive: in science the pure curiosity of the scientist may be mingled with a desire for some technological benefit to be secured by the research. The desire and hope of such explorations are personal qualities of the thinker, and may involve him in a way of life which includes personal sacrifice of less attractive ends, and some measure of abstinence from physical satisfactions. 'To scorn delights and live laborious days', for some purpose of discovery, involves the person of the searcher in his intellectual project, and a weakness of personality will hinder its accomplishment. In other words *the thinker matters*.

When the object of thought is aesthetic or artistic the personality of the thinker becomes of far greater importance. Genius is not a result of determined painstaking, though its expression often involves this. It proceeds from some sensitivity of insight or imagination, from some highly developed sight or hearing or taste, or rhythmic sense, or consciousness of form, or synthetic comprehension, which appear in the first place to be natural gifts, though, before they can be expressed, they require some degree of cultivation. Here the personal element becomes of the highest importance to the thought.

Again it is a commonplace that desire has a powerful effect in shaping thought and its expression. A man's opinions and decisions are seldom impersonal. Without perhaps realizing it, the substance and expression are moulded by subconscious intentions and wishes. These not only positively shape the thinker's processes, but they exclude from his purview elements which a more balanced synthesis would take into account. Even in philosophies which ought to be free and impersonal, the temperament of the thinker is reflected in his thinking. Zeno, Epicurus, Plato and Spinoza could not have produced their systems without being the men they were, and this would account for the illumination given by anecdotes about their lives by such writers as Diogenes Laertius. If this happens in philosophy how much more is it likely to be seen in other disciplines. In theology for example the strange temperament of St. Paul pervades his writings; the gentle melancholy of Boethius, the impetuous intemperance of Tertullian, the introspective depth of Augustine, the quiet commonsense of Hooker, and the ardent turbulence of Luther, condition their theologies and their reasoning with obvious insistence. The man cannot be divorced from his thought: the thought cannot be evaluated without the man.

Not only feeling, but also will is involved in personal thinking. A great deal of thought involves attention: the effort of sustained meditation is felt by some as a severe discipline, and in most cases requires conditions which are favourable to it. Distractions and irrelevant ideas constantly intrude and must be banished by an effort. Sometimes too the will to find a solution affects the thought processes, and reduces or glosses over objections which should be more carefully weighed. A predilection in the thinker, such as the will to adhere to a certain theological position, may easily mould his argument: this is very evident in writers whose known allegiances indicate beforehand the type of conclusion which will be reached, though the writer may imagine himself to be setting out on an unbiased enquiry. To characterize such predispositions as merely 'bliks' is scarcely fair, because in most cases they are rationally grounded. Yet some predispositions are created not by past reasoning, but by environment and upbringing which have conditioned a personal outlook almost beyond redemption. An outstanding example of this is the antithesis between a Catholic and a Protestant outlook on religion, resulting in an almost ineradicable bias.

Imperfect knowledge is undoubtedly the main cause of defects in the conclusions of human thinkers. Socrates believed it to be the sole cause of ethical errors. In past science, false conclusions are gradually yielding to accurate information, but even today a new factual discovery can revolutionize a whole field of thought, as happened in the case of Newtonian physics. It would scarcely be necessary to emphasize this point were it not that so much theology of the past has been based on false cosmology. The shock of the realization that much of the language which has been used about the existence of God, the incarnation of Christ, Heaven, Hell and eschatology is at the least pictorial and at most mythological, has not yet been absorbed by the Churches. The question whether true conceptions can still be conveyed through statements which are empirically unjustifiable remains to be considered.

Another characteristic of human thinking is that a general view may be in itself quite consistent and persuasive, and yet be based on too narrow a field of thought, and untrue, not because of logical errors, but because of its limitations, or its basic presuppositions. The philosophy of Henri Bergson might be instanced as one example of this, and that of Hegel as another. Bergson writes as a biologist, and produces a fascinating picture of the evolution of life and of mind, of the nature of time, and of the mysterious *élan-vital* as the ultimate reality. He accounts for the difference between intellectual thinking and intuition, and discounts theology in favour of a developing biological 'control', of the nature of love. He is, however, tied up by his metaphors, depends on the persuasiveness of his pictorial effects, and by-passes the rigours of metaphysical thought.

His onesidedness on biological and descriptive lines is in sharp contrast with the logical absolutism of Hegel which has largely conditioned subsequent philosophy by the revolts which it produced against its metaphysical logic. His basic assumption is that the real is rational and the rational is real.

He wished by the rigour of philosophical thinking to make it scientific, and to show how all thought fits into a logical scheme of development. The net result is a colourless rational development in which contrasts are brought into synthesis, and falsity is only misapprehended truth, and necessary for its development. The individual person disappears in the evolution of self-conscious spirit, and God becomes the Absolute. The worship of the rational has excluded the importance of the event in itself, or the thing in itself, or the person in himself. The synthesizing function of the mind has become all in all: we cannot see the trees for the wood.

Perhaps these two outstanding examples may suffice to remind us that human thinking, however clear logically, or persuasive pictorially, is often limited by its scope. This is not to claim that a thinker must have omniscience! Leibniz was, perhaps, the last philosopher who could claim to have acquired all the knowledge of his day; since then it has become impossible. But this impossibility imposes a limitation on human thought, which Hegel would not have accepted, namely that no one can claim to think *ex specie aeternitatis* in the full sense, and that the area of our knowledge and experience must colour and limit all our speculations.

Emotional trends of personality also have a powerful effect

on a human thinker. Intense love of nature conditions the thought of Wordsworth, personal disappointment and bitterness colour the satire of Swift, a violent inner conflict dominated Tolstoy's production, over-sensitive religious introspection unbalanced Kierkegaard, pessimism dominated Schopenhauer, and others, Nietzsche was obsessed by egotism; the list could easily be lengthened; hatred, sex-obsession, pietism and ambition have all their victims. Few indeed have achieved the serenity of Sophocles or Goethe, or the wide humanism of Shakespeare or Homer. Often, indeed, the passion has made the writer, as in the case of Sappho and Catullus.

I have instanced only writers in emphasizing the effect of personality on thinking. But of course these are only typical of what is universal. Impersonal and unbiased thought is a rare phenomenon. And it is equally noteworthy that the objects of thought, whether physical or conceptual, are seen differently from almost every personal viewpoint. To emphasize this is scarcely necessary. A tree will be seen with different eyes by a forestry-expert, a bird-lover, an artist, a timber merchant, a lover, a farmer, a botanist, a philosopher, a gardener, a child and a landscape artist. In another category of thought the conceptions evoked in the members of a congregation by an article of the Creed, such as 'I believe in the Holy Ghost' or 'in the Holy Catholic Church' will have at best a superficial similarity but actually a wide variety. A car today, so constant an object of thought, has meanings so different to those concerned with it as almost to defy classification. Mass communication, and especially advertising, endeavour to impose mass meanings and create mass desires. But underneath the similarities thus created there lies a great variety of personal meaning which is only grouped, and superficial. In the solution of problems and questions too, the thought of individuals will present a bewildering variety of conclusions. Everyone has some concern with the economic problems of today, and most thoughtful people have some ideas as to how they might be solved or alleviated. But here again *quot homines tot sententiae*. Even a written foundation document like the Bible, which might be expected to create a certain uniformity of approach, does nothing of the sort. Every religious crank finds in it some justification of his opinions, and every theologian or critic some foundation for his views. The most ultimate of questions—the nature of God—meets at present with such a variety of answers that believers are reduced to a cynic echemythia, revived by Wittgenstein, and a kind of agnostic faith. This will not bear the weight of institutional religion.

Finally the human situation conditions human thinking to an extent not always realized. Our transitory situation between birth and death creates a framework of 'beginning' and 'end' which has an almost universal application. We seek for a beginning and end of the world almost inevitably. We cannot conceive eternity of time or illimitability of space except symbolically in mathematics. Space and time are separate in normal thinking, though the process of evolution requires a conception of space–time, or four dimensional thinking. The Quantum theory seems to require even five dimensions.

Indeed our ways of thought seem to be incurably teleological. Since our own activities are normally directed by purposes, purposelessness has become for us almost equivalent to meaninglessness. We think of God necessarily as having an overriding purpose for his world, undaunted by the fact that to have a purpose means to be dealing with an unknown future, and some forms of obstruction. According to some theological thinkers, eschatology must be a dominant category: providence seems to be an essential characteristic of God. Analogy from the human situation plays a large part in the discernment of the divine. Whether these views are right or wrong is not our present concern. They are instanced to point out that there are definite limitations of human thinking which impose themselves necessarily. We think in an area of present illumination between past darkness which can only be partially explored, and future darkness which can only be dimly penetrated. We think from the viewpoint of one mind in an enveloping mystery of unknown dimensions, and although our horizons are extending vastly by the co-operation of other human thinkers and discoverers, each extension of knowledge seems only to open new perspectives of the infinitely small and infinitely great. We still have to live with limited human capacities in limited spheres of action. Most people are content within these surface actualities of ordinary life. But those who seek to know more about the inner nature of personal life, its sub-conscious and unconscious underground, are baffled also by an infinity of introspection which emphasizes the truth of Heraclitus' gnome of long ago. 'However deeply you search you will never find the limits of the soul.'[1] The psychological aspects of this search are well known: the existential aspects have, as we have seen, raised a doubt as to whether the whole normal processes of subject–object thinking may not be an escape from vital realities, and only the temporary expression of inauthentic existence in this world. Personal thinking suffers from limitations no less serious than those which we have already observed in abstract, existential and theological thought. So far it may well seem that St. Paul has said the last word 'βλέπομεν γὰρ ἄρτι δι' ἐσόπτρου ἐν αἰνίγματι.'

[1] Fr. 71 ap. Diog. IX. 7.

8

HUMAN THINKING IN GENERAL

We have examined the principal types of human thought, rational or metaphysical, existential, theological, mystical and scientific and found limitations in every type. In theology, it is true, we have only considered the efforts of certain thinkers to accommodate it to what is called the modern outlook; the limitations which we have observed in these are not the whole story, because the question of revealed truth has not been considered. Their solutions, however, have rightly been taken into account, because their thinking is essentially human in its attempt to meet the analytical and existential approaches and yet retain what they can of the Christian position. We have seen that abstract rational thinking depends ultimately for content on a concept of the philosopher or an empirical intuition such as that of Being or Substance, that it reduces the thinker, in its pure form, to a mere locus of thought, ignoring his personality, and that in its application to the objective world its concepts are too fluid for general agreement, e.g. the terms 'evolution' or 'religion' or 'immortality'.

Existential thinking has been seen as giving insights into the human situation, but little or no guidance for living, as we do, in an objective world, only to be understood by normal subject–object thought. Further, although it gives religious insights it is irretrievably self-centred and ignores the fact that the individual is also a social being whose life in the world is as important a part of him as his 'self-understanding' and may be equally authentic. And thirdly we have seen scientific thought as incapable of answering ultimate questions or giving any but physical values of a verifiable type: it has no objective except greater knowledge and control of our environment, and has no idea of where it is going: in itself, and apart from other aspects of the scientist's personality, it leads to atrophy of any faculties of the soul except those of sense perception. Mysticism, we saw, provides no answer to the general need of knowledge of God, or to the problem of presenting it to a secular world. Its operation is supra-intellectual and trans-religious. And finally the common-sense thought of the average man is so much involved with his feelings, his will and his special interests or imperfect knowledge that its conclusions carry no general conviction, if he theorizes at all.

There is, however, one obvious characteristic about all thinking, namely that it is 'about' something. Even the existentialist, who decries subject–object thought, makes his existential insights the object of a philosophical attitude when he reflects upon them. The scientist thinks about the physical world, the metaphysician thinks about the whole range of being in the light of a central concept.

Secondly all thinking proceeds from the mind of an individual person however much he may try to make his thoughts abstract, impersonal and such as other rational people must accept. It is an activity of understanding which proceeds from the mind of a person who is himself immersed in the process which he tries to understand, or concerned with a part or parts of it, or seeking self-understanding within it. And it is not only thus space-conditioned, but also time-conditioned in being directed to future purpose or discovery.

Since thinking thus takes place from within the space–time process and is about some object which the thinker selects, it requires a background of personal experience or even of conviction before it can be effective. Its characteristic is rationality, for reason is the instrument by which the mind reaches conclusions and commends them to other thinkers. Reason cannot spin an understanding out of its own processes simply because they are instrumental and not objective, instrumental for an understanding of the objective. Thinking must take place *from* a background of personal being and *about* a presented object of some kind. Christians call the ultimate ground of personal being God, and of presented objects, Creation. Without enquiring as to the meaning of these two terms, we may reasonably here conclude that as *names* for the basic generative power of personal thought and action, and the basic ground of objectivity they are indispensable. To deny that these two terms stand for meaningless non-entities is close to the madness of solipsism, for to deny any subjective reality behind all thinkers is to leave each individual conscious only of his own thinking, and to deny any objective reality as a ground of the objects of thinking is to leave the individual with only objects originating in his own mind.

So far therefore we posit 'God' as the ground of personal being, and the 'Creation' as the ground of objectivity, and both of them as 'other' than the individual thinker. The word 'creation' is, perhaps, unhappily chosen: for so far we have shown no connection between the subjective and the objective grounds of being. These might well be two realities. Berkeley's attempt to avoid this duality by supposing that all our objective experience consists of ideas presented by God to human minds makes nonsense of the scientific exploration of pre-history when there were no thinkers and undoubtedly existing objects. It is near lunacy to suggest that God presents pre-history ready made to a modern scientist, but presented erroneous ideas of pre-history to scientists of the past. Besides, who shall decide, and how, between for example the ideas of Creation presented to a devout fundamentalist and to a cosmological scientist unless God is allowing one or the other to be deceived.

The widely spread logical argument that the idea of God is strictly meaningless, because it can be given no intelligible content, or test of verifiability, is inapplicable to a conception of God as the ground of subjective reality, because meaning is an objective content of minds. If God is the living ground or background of personality his nature cannot be communicated to us objectively. Any assumed objective knowledge of him can only be deduced by us from empirical evidence, on the assumption of creation as due to him, or, of course, from revelation, if revelation is accepted. The attempt thus to give content to God as object of thought would therefore depend on two assumptions both unacceptable to empiricists, namely that God is 'Maker of Heaven and Earth' and that God has revealed himself. On empirical lines no meaningful content can be given for God as objective, and, if truth depends on logical empiricism only, the hypothesis of his existence is probably unnecessary. Further, existence normally implies being in space and time which is necessarily limited by other existents: and neither Christian belief nor scientific research would claim that God exists in this sense. To say that God is real, as distinct from existent, is a different matter; that which is 'behind' or 'the ground of' personal being is at least as real as that which is the basis of the objective world.

9

PRESUPPOSITIONS OF THE APPROACH

THE element of personal perspective through which human thinking takes place is missing from the five modes of thought which we have considered, and yet as we have said each of the great philosophers has elaborated his system through a personal perspective which has given it colour and character. In most cases this perspective is largely conditioned by the *zeitgeist* or contemporary world outlook of the thinker. This element is excluded in intention as a rule but is none the less influential. Yet metaphysical thinking tries to exclude it, Mysticism of course rejects it, Existential thinking buries itself in primary individual insights which are none the less conditioned, as for example by post-war disillusionment, Scientism professedly has none of it, yet each scientist is conditioned by the colour of the scientific atmosphere of his day, and theology, though basing itself on reason and revelation, is notoriously susceptible to the spirit of the age in which it is written.

In the thinking of men and women on practical and speculative subjects generally the perspective becomes far more obtrusive. I, with my general make up and experience, think about a world problem like the Vietnam war, or racial equality about which I try to grasp the main aspects through a perspective which is usually that of my nation or social status, or political views or religion and seldom, if ever, is purely objective and impartial. It is this element that usually causes a breakdown in dialogue.

The *tertium quid*, the perspective through which a thinker regards the object of his thought, is usually neglected, although plainly apparent when it is noticed. It is both individual and general, and is particularly noticeable in theological writing. An interpretation which ignores it is out of touch with its age, and therefore liable itself to be ignored. In any theology worth reading this *Zeitgeist* does not determine the content. But it must colour the interpretation because otherwise it will be hopelessly out of touch. Theology is not, of course, a purely intellectual affair: it is directed towards Christians with the object of confirming or illuminating their faith. Their needs are profoundly affected by the general world-outlook of their age, or if this is too wide, of their national and social environment. The perspective through which the theologian sees his problems is therefore of the highest importance, and an attempt to estimate it is a necessary prelude to any consideration of restatement of belief. He must approach them against a common background of his age.

One must therefore summarize the general attitude of the non-theological yet basically Christian man towards the divine–human situation as he sees it, and think through this perspective towards his needs. I am of course speaking of his theological and not of his spiritual and moral needs, though beliefs should harmonize with these.

What can the theologian take for granted as the perspective of those for whom he writes? Needless to say it is also in a measure a perspective which he shares sympathetically and through which he directs his efforts towards a modern understanding of age-long truths. The aim of this work is not to convince unbelievers, but to present the Christian faith in a form in which it can be firmly held by those who are perturbed and shaken by recent doubts and speculations. Its approach is therefore that of *fides quaerens intellectum*—a typically Anglican one, which, thank God, is possible in our communion. The approach is through a perspective of what the writer feels is demanded in a twentieth-century presentation of the faith on his side, and to the perspective of the modern non-theological Christian, whose attitude may be summarized somewhat as follows:

(1) He believes in God as Creator, Judge, and in some way transcendent or at least high above us;

(2) He believes in Christ as perfect man, sent by God to save and redeem from sin. He is to be called Son of God though in what sense is uncertain.

(3) He believes in the Holy Spirit as a power for goodness opposing spiritual evils.

(4) He regards the Holy Trinity as a mystery for theologians.

(5) He looks on the Church as a society of Christians for worship, fellowship, teaching and upholding moral principles, but is puzzled by its hierarchy and organization, though prepared to support them as part of a necessary institution.

(6) He regards theology with distant respect and a suspicion that much of it is out-of-date.

(7) He venerates Holy Scripture as an inspired record and guide though conditioned by the outlook of the periods in which it was written, fallible in details, and rightly subject to criticism.

(8) He feels that the modern world badly needs a spiritual corrective. Christian belief and practice, he thinks, best supply this need.

(9) He regards the scientific exploration of the world as apart from religion; beliefs in providence, heaven and hell are only in a dim background. Faith is more of the nature of personal trust and optimism, than of belief—and grace is simply believed as 'God helping' without theological grounds.

(10) The future is unknown, but somehow in God's hands. Apprehension about it is more prevalent than faith, because of present human failures.

(11) Miracles are doubted. Sin is regarded less seriously because psychological and social educational cures are thought to be progressing. Crime causes more anxiety.

(12) Religion generally is valued for the personal stability which it gives. Differences of Churches are less acutely felt. Christianity it is thought must be more extravert, not so much, as formerly, in evangelism, but in social

service. Intensity of religious life is admired, but the general aim of Christians is a good life in society, sustained by religious practice.

(13) He accepts that doctrine must often be supernatural but prefers that it be understandable.

This perspective is not a 'Blik' but a body of belief sincerely held through which an average Christian looks at his problems and at his theology. It now remains to be considered how, through such a perspective, the doctrinal beliefs of the Church may be reunderstood in the twentieth century. The progress of philosophical thought, of scientific knowledge, and of historical study—not to mention many other aspects, make a reconstruction inevitable. If it cannot yet be expressed in formularies of a united church, it may at least provide interpretations to which assent can be given, as an interim *confessio fidei*.

PART TWO

PROLOGUE TO PART TWO

AS preface to the treatment of Christian doctrines which follows an explanation of the principles on which I have worked is due to the reader, particularly if he is one of those who still believe that unintelligibility in any central doctrine is a positive advantage since it adds mystery and demands greater faith. More rational presentation of the arcana of religion, if not condemned as blasphemous, is labelled as heretical: and rationalizing of religious truths is not only deemed irreverent, but also dangerous, as suggesting that natural and revealed religion have anything in common. It is almost as though faith in the irrational is necessary for salvation.

As against such obscurantism—such as Karl Barth expressed when he said 'Belief cannot reason with unbelief; it can only preach to it', my contention is that if an approach to central Christian beliefs can be found which, without diminishing their content, can make them more comprehensible, the gain in attracting people of intelligence will be greater than the loss of those whose faith is on the lines of Tertullian's *credibile est quia ineptum est: certum est quia impossible*. Faith is not, in spite of St. Augustine, a supernatural *gift* of God: although evoked by prevenient Grace, it is a self-projection into personal trust from grounds established as sufficiently reasonable to justify the leap. It was on the grounds of his already revealed power and holiness that Christ asked for faith in himself. It is neurotic to describe faith as Kierkegaard did as a 'passionate inwardness' embracing objective uncertainty, as a leap into paradox. It can be such on isolated occasions, and in times of great stress. But not normally, and people generally are normal; part of their normality is refusal to commit themselves irrationally.

Accordingly, it is a postulate of my approach, which may be observed particularly in the chapter on the Atonement, that if the same homiletic end or spiritual conviction can be achieved by a more comprehensible explanation we are justified in preferring it to a less comprehensible, provided always that the full truth of the revelation is not minimized.

My second presupposition has already been indicated. God transcendent, living, and radiant is beyond our comprehension in his essential being, but has constantly revealed what can be known or what needs to be known, of himself by mediated action, recognized by mankind as his. Such revelations as he has given through his Logos, or self-revealing activity, have been received by men and understood through the thought-background of their age. Religious thinking is not metaphysical or existential, but symbolical. The appropriate symbols have been provided by the generation which received the revelation. Thus for example a concentration of spiritual evil has been symbolized as a devil and a sense of a present spirit of holiness as an angel. The ages provide their symbols, each in its own terms, often without any realization that they are symbolic. Later ages recognize that the actions or impulses of God have been so mediated, and understand their meaning as, for example, we would now understand 'Lamb of God'.

Since many elements of Christian worship descend to us from remote ages (and incidentally it may be said that this is perhaps an important reason for calling Christianity an historical religion) the symbols are mixed into hymns and prayers and ritual generally so indiscriminately that they cannot now be sorted out. Nor should they be, because our faith is not a special twentieth-century Christianity, but a continuance, in which past and present are blended both in human history and in heaven. God reveals himself progressively as man can understand: man interprets his revelations progressively in terms of his age: *heilsgeschichte* is not history but a living continuum of symbolic interpretation pervading the historical scene.

One further point should be considered in deference to analytical philosophers. Can true conceptions be conveyed through statements which are not empirically justifiable? Obviously true empirical statements cannot be so conveyed. But these are statements about verifiable space–time events or situations. They are purely factual.

Now there is a wide range of personal factual statements which are not verifiable and yet are normally accepted as true. For example 'I have a headache', 'I am very sorry', 'I am terrified'. These are personal disclosure statements; we have no privileged access to other people's feelings or thoughts. If they are to be taken as true, they will only be acceptable if some cognate action follows, for example growing pale, going to bed, giving assistance, taking cover. Personal statements to be accepted as true must be revealed by actions or observable changes.

Since the divine revelation is personal in the highest degree it has to be made to us in word or deed. If the word, of a prophet for example, is to be believed it will carry in itself an authentic convincingness reinforced by the known sincerity and devotion of the prophet. Revelation by deed, however, will have to secure conviction by being beyond normal experience, i.e. mysterious, super-human, miraculous, uncanny or otherwise unaccountable. That there are such experiences of a genuine kind is essential for Christian belief. Of course some are otherwise explicable. And if a reasonable or scientific human explanation is acceptable we should prefer it, on the principle of not using a steam hammer to kill a mouse. But if super-human qualities or actions are unmistakably manifested and convey an inspiration such we can only call divine we are justified in assuming them to be true revelations from the source of truth. Revelation by deed is essential for belief in a living Creator and Lord, and is a necessary supplement to the inherent convincingness of the revealed word.

In worship we leave the factual, and transport ourselves into the symbolic, knowing that the symbolic coherent system of our faith is in its own sense historical, and truer than fact, because it describes God's eternal, living, spiritual, activity towards us as man can best describe and comprehend it.

1

THE NEW TESTAMENT

THE thought-background into which the new revelation of God in Christ was received was quite definitely Jewish, that of the Old Testament. This was the personal perspective through which the new factors were thought out. The creation of a New Testament by the christian Church gives us an impression of a water-shed in world history, an abrupt division between an old dispensation and a new. This is most misleading. Christ and his disciples moved and taught in a Jewish milieu. His contemporaries, if they were Jews, thought of him as an unorthodox rabbi whose preaching and miracles made him famous or notorious, a rebel against the 'establishment'—the priesthood, pharisees and scribes: some hoped to find in him a revolutionary leader and were disappointed and disillusioned by his death: some regarded him in some sense as a hope of Israel, and his disciples began to wonder whether he might not even be the promised Messiah: in fact he seems to have encouraged this belief, whether or not he explicitly claimed the title. Many learned to love him. More were astonished by his miracles, and impressed by his authoritative teaching. His crucifixion seemed to end vain hopes—'We trusted that it had been he which should have redeemed Israel.'[1]

That was virtually all till after the resurrection. It was then that the thinking began. Up to this the Jewish background was all, and it was into this framework of revealed religion, the presupposition of Jewish thinking, that the new revelation of God had to be fitted. Hence the *kerygma*, or first proclamation of the new Gospel. 'The time is fulfilled. The saviour promised by God in the prophets has come, even Jesus of Nazareth, whom the Jewish rulers handed over to the Romans

[1] Luke 19. 21.

to be crucified, whom God raised from the dead. He will return from Heaven to judge the world in righteousness. Repent and believe the Gospel, and you will receive forgiveness of your sins.'

The revelation of God in Christ had to be understood at first through the medium of Hebrew religion. Jesus as God's revelation of himself must be 'son' of God: he was known as man therefore he had to be born as man, yet not as man. He had to descend from, and ascend to, heaven; he had to be linked with Moses and Elijah, the law and the prophets, and be attested by voices from heaven. His followers were to be the new Israel of God, purified by a new Passover sacrifice and covenant. His expected return was linked with Jewish apocalyptic speculations. He had placed himself within and yet above the old religion, and by it he had to be understood.

Students of the Bible have been convinced at all times that this was really God's plan for the world. And certainly no higher revelation of it has been given than what we find in the Old and New Testaments. Religion is not philosophy. Sacred history is based on religious insights which no scientific historian could entertain. Christian developments of Old Testament themes have been continuous: imagery has changed, new truths like the activity of God's Spirit, the nature of the Church, and of sacramental grace have been divined. But the process has been evolutionary and elements not contained in the Judaic tradition have been incorporated. The old symbols pointed to truths, but new truths required new symbols which yet must harmonize with the old. The first Christians had virtually no other symbols to use for religious expression: hence, in large measure, the continuity.

An interesting example of this is to be found in the story of the nativity. When Jesus was recognized as the Lord, divine, sent by God, the first interpretation of him was Messiah—sent from heaven. How was he 'sent'? The disciples had known him as man: he must have been born as man: and he must have been of Davidic descent, that was, of the family of Joseph.

His mother Mary was known, of course. Joseph was his father legally. But God was his father: he had come down from heaven. The double strain could be understood if there was a miraculous conception by Mary from the spirit of God, and if Joseph 'feared not to acknowledge' her as his wife, and legalize his son, though he had to be represented as conceived 'before they came together'.[1] Hence the Messiah was at once from God and legally a descendent in the royal line, and Mary's conception was virginal, and from God, not man. In the setting in which God in Christ was realized the 'Virgin Birth' was necessary: a true symbol. Another early explanation taught that God 'took possession' of Jesus at his baptism—a belief possibly caused by the difficulty of a virginal conception. The certainty that Jesus was divine, though human, created the explanations. The Virgin Birth was true symbolically, and exalted pure womanhood with a symbolism that was also true. Given God 'in heaven' and 'Son of God' as true symbols, given a belief in God's special revelation of himself through Israel, given the certainty of real manhood in Jesus, and a belief in the holiness of motherhood and the family as the centre of social stability, no religious statement in a context of worship could be symbolically truer than the story of the nativity of Christ. A religious statement is not a philosophical statement; man cannot worship abstractions. It is not a factual or even a necessarily historical statement: because these mean only what they state. It is not a myth, because a myth is man-made and not revealed. It is what we find all through Holy Writ, a god-given symbol for human worship and guidance: and the means by which it is appropriated (and indeed rationally assimilated) is faith.

The symbols are the Veil, the living picture upon which divine truth is projected for man's understanding.

The stories encircling the event of the nativity, the star, the angel-chorus, and the visit of the magi are artistically perfect and have a legendary air. They cannot be believed as factual,

[1] Matt. I. 18, 25.

and yet their appropriateness and beauty are unquestionable. Like many of the parables, and a number of Old Testament stories, like parts of the Apocalypse, and some of the prophetic visions, they bear the marks of divine artistry such as often marks the perfections of natural beauty. If this is so, how was it communicated? The parables are *sui generis* and need no explanation except that God was in Christ. God's artistry expressed itself in the story form of his revelation. Other stories may well be visions, like Ezekiel's or that of the Transfiguration. Others like the giving of the law to Moses and the star of the magi may have had some factual basis round which gathered an inspired folk-lore. Simple piety can embroider a glowing tapestry on a thin pattern of event. It is not deliberate myth making, but the accretion from religious imagination. Its truth is accepted uncritically and passed on, not without adornment, by a simple faith. The growth of symbolic truth is multifarious, but the process need not vitiate its spiritual origin and meaning. As understanding progresses some symbols lose their creditability and value and become obsolete because God ceases to inspire or speak through them. Man does not need them because he has received a more appropriate symbolism. The 'tables of the law' were appropriate in a time when codes were inscribed on stone and could well be believed. By the time of St. Paul they had become 'the fleshly tables of the heart'.[1] The 'rushing mighty wind and tongues of fire'[2] given at Pentecost was an intermediate stage between God in the flames of Sinai and the 'blessed unction from above' which is 'comfort, life and fire of love'. The factual feeding of the five thousand has become the eucharistic actuality of the bread of life. The actual passover lamb passed through the Passover feast into the sacrifice of Calvary and thence to be the supreme token of divine and sacrificial love. As spiritual understanding deepens, the meaning of the God-given symbols becomes more vital than their original factuality. New perspectives change the discernment of the truth behind the

[1] 2 Cor. 3. 3. [2] Acts 2. 2, 3.

symbols but it is still believed. Man-made symbolisms and myths which have not God behind them fade out, like the Olympian Gods or fairy lore.

Just as the dissection of a corpse in a medical school gives multiple information as to the constitution of a physical body and how it was articulated but can give no knowledge of the living person whose body it was, so the historical and critical dissection of the gospels can give much information as to how they were composed and formed, but can tell little or nothing of the living person who, as it were, inhabited them and gave them life. The quest of the historical Jesus is now said to have failed, probably rightly. But the living personality who shone through the Gospels and caused them to be written stands behind and apart from the critical dissection. And, from another point of view, a history of the Napoleonic period might conceivably be written without any reference to Napoleon himself: yet he would have to be inferred. So a history of Europe might be written without reference to Christ: but the picture would demand him as accounting for what else would be inexplicable.

The corpus of New Testament literature is unique: the Gospels themselves are unique in literature. Their power has been such, that some personal and divine source seems to be an inevitable conclusion. Those who stumble at the word 'divine' as mythological are atheist, because 'ground of being' and 'basic reality' are metaphysical concepts, and 'love' is only one of the values known to mankind. Neither atheism nor theism can be proved empirically. But theism covers a far wider field of human experience, which is not all sense experience. When events in the space–time series are impregnated by divine action, their expression for humanity must be in symbolic terms. For a symbol not only belongs to our world but partakes of the reality which it symbolizes.

2

THE BEING OF GOD

THE revelation of the divine name to Moses in Exod. 3. 14, 'I AM THAT I AM' or simply as 'I AM', the being One, has a profound significance. Not only does it assert the personality of God, but it removes him completely from the range of the objective. God is 'the speaker', his name is not conferred, it indicates no characteristic, and gives no handle, like other names. This insight into, or revelation of, the divine being is, as we have already suggested, hyper-subjective. It is transcendent not in the sense of 'out there' but as super-personal. Super-personal is not quite the right phrase, for it suggests what some theologians have said of God that he is at least personal, and may be more. What this 'more' could be is left undefined. Rather the divine name suggests an intense burning reality of personal life, of which human persons are only a faint reflection. We can justifiably argue analogically towards God from the noblest aspects of human subjective and personal activity, but we cannot say, for example, that love, justice and wisdom are characteristics of his 'nature'. We can only realize our active loving, or being just, or showing wisdom as pointing to a personal lover, to one who is all-just, all-wise and all-loving.

Our approach to the being of God cannot be described as intuitive since that would imply a kind of looking into ourselves and exalting our best qualities into a conception of his greatness. It is, rather, a vital experience, which can only partially be described. When we experience beauty in nature or art it is partly because in seeing the object our sensitivity is aroused to a sense of satisfaction: but at the same time we experience a feeling that the reaction aroused in us is inadequate; that the appreciation is less intense than it could be:

we feel that there is a subjective and personal appreciation that is more intense and deeper than ours. The inadequacy of our personal experience and the realization of its inadequacy has, as its background, an imagined perfection of beauty-experience which could be real and in us is only partially realized. The same is true of love-experience. It is a common experience of lovers not only that they cannot express what they feel, but also that what they feel is inadequate: that, because they are what they are, their best loving falls short of what love could be in a perfect lover. The fact that the laying down of life itself is the greatest love that can be shown by man, indicates the impossibility for a living human being of showing all that love can be. The case of knowledge is even clearer: as a scholar plunges more deeply into his subject he realizes more acutely the inadequacy of his knowing: it is not the greatness of the area of knowledge that daunts him, but the limitation of his power of knowing it; he is a knower of limited powers, and in this he falls short of what knowing could be in an all comprehending mind.

In these matters the sense of our powers as finite is not brought to us by contrast with any assumed infinite. Infinity leaves us cold, and no one worries because he cannot reach it. The contrast which humbles us is between our vital function in appreciating, knowing or loving and that of an aesthete, a knower or a lover in whom these active excellences function perfectly. God is the Being in whom the personal vital activities exist in this perfection, and are active qualities which affect us inter-personally, and not infinite stores which he possesses. The wrongness of the latter conception comes out in the often debated crux of divine omniscience and human freedom. Omniscience is conceived objectively as a vast store of all knowledge, past, present and future somehow 'possessed' by the mind of God. In face of such detailed knowledge of our future actions free will is felt to be impossible, and theologians have attempted to wriggle out of the dilemma in various ways, e.g. that God's omniscience, being eternal, knows how we will act, although temporally our will is our own and free. The mistake lies in thinking of omniscience as an objective possession of the mind of God. What it really means is that the activity of knowing in God is perfectly performed whenever he exercises his personal power of understanding. The appeal to his knowledge in prayer is an appeal to one whose knowing of our situation, *when we ask for it or state it*, responds with perfect judgment and clarity. But his attention and power of knowing all our needs and circumstances needs to be made effective to us by claiming or acknowledging it: then, even if we misrepresent ourselves and our situation, his discernment knows the truth.

To say that God is at least personal because he 'possesses' personal qualities is not enough. For at once the statement objectifies God and we have to go on to ask 'does he exist'? What we should say is that as the power behind our personal qualities there is a Person in whom they are active perfectly. The question is not whether he is a real person, but whether we are. Our personal life is a mixture of reality and existence: existence is temporal, finite, and in many ways unreal, even before it ceases to be. It is more of a potentiality than a reality: it is wrong by the absence of rightness, evil by the absence of goodness, earthbound by the absence of contact with the divine. Only Christ could say I am the way, the truth and the life, because in him the reality of the divine life was always active.

We are so used to thinking of God objectively that we miss his reality. We catalogue his attributes and think that this is knowledge of him, precise knowledge. But when we try to think of him as object the attributes vanish into a vague haze of glory centring on a great circle of undifferentiated light, which means little more than 'sun of my soul'. The true way is to realize in our personal life the glorious vitalities of which he is the source, the living source. He is our life, potentially, and we cannot think of our life as object: we can only feel it as real in so far as it proceeds from the vital reality of God.

God is not merely personal, but a person. The reason why some theologians have chosen to call God 'personal-plus' and have shrunk from calling him a person is because they think that to be a person involves limitation and finiteness. They think of 'a person' as being like all the other persons whom we see and know as finite existents. They think of other persons objectively—i.e. as centres of consciousness whom we know at particular times and places. But personality is different from a man's local and temporary existence. The existent human being may be involved in space and time, and conditioned by his body and environment. But his personality is not local or temporal, except in so far as he is earthbound. Personality is in a different category of thought. An enquirer about John Smith, for example, might be told of his physique, habits, work, dwelling place, career, friends and relatives and so on. But if he went on to ask about the space–time whereabouts of his personality there could be no answer, because personality is not so localized: it is in a different category from the factual and describable. If we think introspectively of our own personalities we cannot conceive them as objective: they are real; in depth they seem to transcend our factual knowledge of ourselves. As mortals we are bound into space–time conditions but there is always a consciousness of partially transcending these conditions by some affinity with a greater reality than mere existence; we feel that our life is not wholly earthbound and finite. Personality is not measurable in those terms. To be a person is something greater than to be an individual.

Thus God, as a Person, differs from human persons qualitatively. His life differs from ours by intensity of reality. The difference is not assessable in any terms other than those of life and spirit. His nature is a living intensity of personal being, and we can realize him as a person of entire perfection without any idea that to be a person involves him in finitude. He is a person to whom we can approach personally, in worship, adoration and prayer without thinking of him objectively at all. We know him subjectively in life—categories by what

St. Paul calls ἐπίγνωσις, a discernment which is spiritual rather than mental.[1]

If then God is a person, he is literally one: not one among others, but one in the sense of primal reality. He is 'living' at the source of all personal life: and he is spirit. What then is spirit? It is life but life in its intensest quality and we must not separate πνεῦμα from ψύχη except in terms of a grading of the same reality. Life as proceeding from God is πνεῦμα: but πνευμα can blend with and interpenetrate ζώη, human life, because it is the same in essence. The ζώη of God is πνεῦμα; spirit is the activity of his life. The term which best expresses him is that used by Jesus,—Father: the source of the being of persons. Faith is our approach to him: Grace is his approach to us.

[1] See my article in *C.Q.* Vol. CLIV p. 438, 1953.

3

THE HOLY TRINITY

THE doctrine arose from Jewish monotheism, coupled with first-hand post-resurrection conviction of the Godhead of Christ, and with the vivid experience, which came immediately to believers, of God as active towards them by his spirit. Until the Council of Nicea (A.D. 325) and its amplification at Constantinople (381) and Chalcedon (451) there was no complete agreement on the solution. The relation between the divine persons, and the manner of the union of Godhead and manhood in Christ, were unsettled questions. Acute minds of Greek theologians contended for their own solutions. Councils considered them, either adopting them, or rejecting them as heresies, not always for strictly theological reasons. Agreement was at last reached at Constantinople, but it was reached through the perspective of contemporary Greek thought, with substance as its primary category. The substance underlying the three divine Persons was one and the same: but each Person had his own hypostasis, a word taken to mean that which constitutes personal being.' As Christ had really been made man, the two natures divine and human, each in its fulness, were united in one hypostasis. But the agreed solution had to admit two illogical paradoxes, the Three in one and One in three, and the God–Man. The Fathers, thinking in terms of substance, could see no other solution. To believe in these paradoxes, being intellectually impossible, was considered to be an act of faith. But faith is ultimately personal trust based on a rationally tenable belief and the term is unfairly used if it compels the assertion of intellectual belief in what the intellect must reject by the laws of reason.

The mistake of the pre-Nicene Church was perhaps inevitable because of the term substance; its static nature was unsuitably applied to God, who must be understood in terms of dynamic life. When this is done, the paradoxes vanish. God is a divine person or rather a divine personal life. The category of life or spirit leads to no paradox. The spirit of God is the supreme reality: spirit is not confined to areas of operation, nor separated in such a way as to lead to paradox. The divine reality expresses himself to our understanding in three distinct ways, all of which are personal in character. He expresses himself in terms of 'creation' (see Chap. 4). He expresses himself in Christ as a man whom God possesses. He expresses himself in living personal inspiration: and yet remains always one divine personal spirit. This is not mere modalism, for a mode is only a transitory form of expression: God himself is active as 'father'; God himself is active in the Son; and active also in human lives as personally inspiring. These three manifestations are continuous activities of one personal life. God himself is present and working in all three. It is the same God who is active in three ways which are, to us, so different and yet so same, that we can speak of each as a person of a Triune Godhead, although the distinctness is not hypostatized as in fourth and fifth century thought. The doctrine of the Holy and Blessed Trinity is a doctrine of the Godhead as known to man in three active manifestations.

Jesus spoke of God and to God as 'Father'; he referred to himself as 'son of man' and *seems* to have accepted the title son of God during the incarnation, and it became prevalent after the Resurrection. He also spoke of the Holy Spirit in personal terms. The names were taken too literally by early believers, and thought to indicate three separate and personal beings. Jewish monotheism could not be lightly abandoned: and the result was the paradox of three persons in one Godhead. At first belief was binitarian, and the locus of the Holy Spirit in the Godhead was not established as coequal for some time. When it was, theologians racked their brains in trying to understand the intern economy of the Trinity, and the hypostatic distinction. As each person was God, the attributes of the Godhead must be fully present in each. Yet there must be distinction sufficiently strong to prevent confusion: thus the Father was the 'fount of Godhead', the son was 'only-begotten' and the Holy Ghost was 'proceeding'. Μονογένης was taken to imply eternal generation, whatever that means. And the 'procession' of the Holy Spirit was a safeguard against ideas of inferiority or emanation. The use of 'Spirit of God' in the Old Testament indicated equal eternity, although the personal presence of the Holy Ghost after the Incarnation was felt to be different from that of the spirit of God who 'spake by the prophets'. He is personalized in believers, as the Son was personalized in human form. The mode of procession of the Third Person was later disputed, namely whether he proceeded 'from the Father and the Son' or from the Father through the Son, and the oral tradition of the words of Christ in the gospels was treated almost as a legal document by those in search of proof texts. Further the three hypostases invited speculation as to the internal 'economy' of the Godhead, and the very obscurity of the doctrine was welcomed as consonant with the mystery of God. We certainly know God in three personal manifestations, but this does not necessarily involve three personal beings in the one Godhead. It is the same God who spoke 'at sundry times and in divers manners in times past unto the fathers by the prophets, who in these last days [as they seemed to the writer of Hebrews] hath spoken to us by his Son'[1] and who speaks still through the Holy Spirit. It is quite unnecessary to burden the minds of believers with Trinitarian doctrine which reaches its climax of expression in the Athanasian creed, when it is realized that it all depended on separating what never should have been divided, the one only and true God whom we know as living personal and perfect Being, who has at all times manifested himself as necessary ground of personal reality, as fully shown on earth as Jesus, the man who was God-possessed, and as guiding now

[1] Heb. I. I, 2.

our thoughts and lives by the same Spirit as was incarnate in the Son of Man.

On this understanding little restatement of Christian doctrine is necessary. One might suggest 'I believe in God as Father, God as Son and God as Holy Spirit' and in the Doxology we would ascribe glory to God, Father, Son and Holy Spirit, using the three latter terms together as synonyms for God.

The effect of this on other aspects of doctrine, especially on the doctrine of the Atonement and of the Holy Spirit, will have to be considered. But the removal of the logical stumbling block, the theological explanations of which are so unconvincing, would not diminish the fullness of the faith which sees God active towards mankind in the three personal manifestations.

4

THE DOCTRINE OF CREATION

'IN the beginning God created the Heaven and the Earth: and the earth was without form, and void.' This account permits a possible understanding like Plato's of an ordering by God of a pre-existent chaotic matter. The J.E. account in Gen. 2. 4–25 simply speaks of 'the day that the Lord God made the earth and the heavens'. The P.S. account adds to the catalogue of each phase of creation that God 'saw that it was good'. The generally accepted Christian view of creation is that the world came into being out of nothing by the will of God. Whether creation was in time or simultaneous with time is disputed: the accounts in Genesis are clearly mythological though the religious insight is so remarkable (as in particular in the story of the Fall) as to deserve the name of inspiration. It is possible to read into the six stages of creation a dim idea of evolutionary progress. Christians of the twentieth century read Genesis for its religious value, but turn to science for the truth about primaeval conditions. But science cannot pronounce whether God made the universe or whether it had what could be called a beginning. It can only describe geological and astrological aeons fading backwards into boundless time, without signs of any divine origin. Creation out of nothing, also, is another logical paradox. The fact that our minds think necessarily in terms of beginning and ending, may imply that the ideas of creation and 'the end of the world' are only required by our ways of thinking. God and matter may be aspects of one reality and 'creation' may only mean that the physical universe depends for its reality on God, the ground of Being.

This leaves the question in an unsatisfactory state: we have seen that empirical science can give no evidence for or against the existence of God: nor can it lead us back to any beginning of the universe. And yet the heavens and earth proclaim continually to mankind their goodness, beauty and order. Of course there is disorder too, and perhaps absence of beauty, and various evils. But it seems that man in his handling of his world is *finding* excellences and bringing order; in other words 'seeing that it is good' and drawing out values from what, to pure science, is material fact. The scientist himself is led on by the thrill of discovery and often overwhelmed by wonder at what he finds. Technology applies the finds to human needs; man is finding what Genesis says 'God saw', in his world.

This power of perceiving what is good is highly personal: historically it has emerged from what is good for the self for the tribe, for the city, for the nation and finally 'for mankind'. We have seen God as the living power behind personal qualities, as the person in whom they are active personally. So, as we might expect, our power of perceiving what is good is a faint reflection of God who saw. But God is said to be not only the seer of values in the material universe, but also the creator of what man discovers in it. In Genesis he is the one who said let there *be* light; and there was light. The being of the universe is attributed to him, and not only the seeing of values in the material world. We cannot, for reasons already given, say, with Berkeley, that being is the same as being perceived. The starry heavens were there before any man existed to be thrilled by their beauty. And a person, even a person of perfect qualities, can have no power of creating material: he can shape it, order it, admire it and use it. Yet a limited power of creation in us is perhaps our greatest quality. Creative imagination can produce, as in a novel, characters which seem to come alive, and take charge of their author, who, in great books, is almost watching what they will do. It can produce works of art, buildings, music, machines, but always out of some material, always from forms and ideas which have once been perceived. I had thought at one time that the universe originated from the creative imagination of God and that we are, as it were, creatures of God's dream, just as our dream characters seem to act independently of us. Even though they are the creation of a dreaming mind, we watch what they are doing without any control of what they may do. But imagination's objects are derived from forms and colours and deeds all previously perceived. And the thought of an imagination that can create without any images on which to work seems paradoxical.

Shall we then leave the mysteries of the origin of the universe to the astronomers and physicists, as outside the sphere of theology? This is tempting. We are concerned with religious faith and values, and might well say that it is immaterial for us to know how the universe originated. This would mean that we would abandon speculation on the 'first things' and take the universe as we know it as 'there' and given. Scientists can deal with that. Our task would be to impart order and values into our surroundings, and not to speculate on how they began. In that case Creation would fall out as a theological problem, and be taken as it is given. This would involve a dichotomy between religion and science, religion dealing with spiritual and personal values, and science with objective facts. It would also appear to lead us to posit two first principals, God and Matter, both presumably coeternal. And the belief that this is God's world would be shaken if he did not create it.

Spinoza boldly identified God with nature, seeing 'God' as *natura naturans* and Nature as *natura naturata*—each being the same substance as seen in two 'attributes', extension and thought. Bertrand Russell has something of the same idea, when he suggests that events appear to us in two series, psychological and physical, though they are themselves neutral. But he takes his 'atomic particulars' as given: and can derive from them no hint of any God.

With these two suggestions we should also consider St. Paul's insight in 1 Cor. 2. 12–13. 'We did not receive the spirit of the world, but the spirit that proceeds from God, that we might know God's gracious gifts to us. And it is of these that we speak, not in scholastic arguments of human wisdom but as we are taught by the Spirit, interpreting spiritual things to those who have been given the spirit [or "in spiritual terms"].' There is here a reference to a type of spiritual discernment, called elsewhere by St. Paul ἐπίγνωσις which is a supplement to rational knowledge and inspired by the Holy Spirit.

If there is such an ἐπίγνωσις or spiritual discernment by which the things of the spirit are known, it brings us back to what I have called Personal thinking, that is a type of thought in which there are three factors, the personality and circumstances of the thinker, the object of his thought and a *tertium quid* referring to a scheme of things or principles of value which he accepts as good and right. For a Christian thinker this principle is, of course, God: and all the discernment due to the conviction of spiritual realities is ἐπίγνωσις—not a higher stage of knowledge like metaphysics, but an illumination effected and affected by the reality of God. The creation story would then be the symbol through which God makes known his 'basicity'.

Scientific thought is rightly content to search backwards for a beginning of things, and to theorize on it from such evidence as it can find. For religious thought based on spiritual discernment there can be no complete world view without the *tertium quid* beyond mind and matter, the divine personal spirit, the ground of being and value. Personal thinking is wrong in trying to import God into the scientific factual picture, as though Creation were a scientific fact of the past. Religious thought needs God as the reality behind the universe and ourselves, but not the Deist God as artificer of the great machine. So the 'doctrine of creation' is really a mythological way of saying 'the earth is the Lord's and all that therein is; the compass of the world and they that dwell therein' (Ps. 14. 1) and 'the Heavens declare the glory of God: and the firmament showeth his handiwork' (Ps. 19. 1). It is not a scientific statement at all: it is based on a spiritual certainty which discerns

God through the natural world because of the values which his spirit enables us to see in it. We too 'see that it is good' but 'in a glass darkly'. A clearer spiritual insight gives a clearer translucency.

Theological thinking in fact takes place in a different context from that of science. Time, space and matter are the background conditions of physical science. Theology has no use for any of these. Its background is the personal reality of an eternal Godhead. It thinks in terms of spiritual values, and personal events. If we ask a theologian about creation he should reply 'I do not know: but neither do scientists: what I do know is that God alone gives it reality, meaning and value'. Is God, then, not the creator of man? We know that man appeared in the course of evolution. If he appeared by God's will, surely that might be called the creation of man? No: what has really made man, as we know him, is a growth in likeness to the divine person, a reaching out of man, marred by many failures, towards God-likeness, inspired by God. This is not teleology: it is an attraction of persons towards and by the Divine person: a coming of man from what he is potentially into the image and likeness of God. Often man mistakes his way to God-likeness: the failures teach him that it does not lie in power, or in self-assertion, because God is not a potentate of earth. The sense of the eternal, the discovery of the higher values, the finding of ways out from imprisonment in individuality, and the realization of God, all draw us out from the temporal and physical here and now, towards a fulness of personal spirit inspired by God. This is not a measurable space–time process. We can only live its development. We may miss the attraction by being so deeply immersed in this life that our eyes are darkened, our ears are deafened, and we fail to realize God. He is really the ground of our being, but we do not find him if we are earth-bound. He is our maker spiritually because our potentiality is drawn out by his attraction. He did not begin us nor does he end us; He simply is, as eternal possibility to which we awaken; his creation of us is the awakening of personality and the drawing. Theology is speaking of God's world and not of ours; we must cease to try to drag creation into it, for if it belongs anywhere it is to the space–time stream. God's world or kingdom is real, but not existent anywhere. It is a kingdom of souls drawn together by Christ, subsisting as an earthly society in the Church. Its being is the life inspired by God. We cannot say how it began or how it will end because it is eternal. The question of how we came into the space–time stream is really one for science to answer if it can. Our concern is with 'I am', and our reality is dependent on the closeness of our being to the great I AM on whom all personal being depends because he gives us such reality as we attain as persons.

Attempts to solve the problem of creation by denying the dualism of mind and matter have been made most notably by the Stoics, Spinoza and Teilhard de Chardin. The Stoics posited a primal material, something like the πῦρ λογικόν of Heraclitus, which was neither mind nor matter, but steered by its indwelling rationality which they called Nature or God or reason. Spinoza boldly said that mind and matter are really the same, God or nature appearing to us in two of his attributes, thought and extension. De Chardin envisages an ensoulment of matter through an evolutionary process into a biosphere and a noosphere and ultimately a pleroma in which Christ will be all and in all. In spite of the logical consistency of Spinoza, and the daring speculation of de Chardin, the Stoics seem to have devised the sanest pantheism. The idea of God working as a ferment within the material and guiding evolution by an inner rationality is attractive. But it depersonalizes God into immanent reason, in spite of their idea of providence. And it is difficult to imagine a primitive mind–matter complex or stuff from which the evolution began.

God is God from everlasting, but the process of human apprehension of his majesty is itself a kind of evolution comparable with that of the material world. To the believer the material world seems sometimes translucent with value and quality which imply a divine origin or basis—yet to the physicist it is electronic or gaseous, and to the philosopher it is a series of organic pattern-events in space-time. For Alexander God emerges from the process in the end, and really depends for his being on it. For Whitehead God is the lure of the process drawing all things to himself and the eternal objects. For Aristotle God is the unmoved mover outside the process, but in a sense directing it through its appetition towards the forms which are the content of his thought. To scientists like Eddington and Jeans the physical world is not self-dependent, and requires some being of the nature of God or Mind to account for it. This is not far from 'and God said, "Let there *be* light" and there was light.' But it is not an explanation—just an hypothesis assumed to be necessary. God can never be an hypothesis.

We have rejected the idea that the physical universe is the creation of the divine imagination, because there can be no imagining or making of images, if there is nothing of which they are images. One would have to posit, with Plato, a realm of eternal forms which God contemplated before he reproduced them in 'matter'. And the fixity of a realm of forms would preclude any real development such as is apparent in the forms of the natural world.

The possibility and prevalence of natural religion seem to show that the universe, as apparent to human senses, appears to point to an author who permits himself to be known dimly through his works. Human scientific explanations of the material world, however, seem to show it as an electronic activity in space and time. This reduction of the material to units of energy could be conceived as expressing the power aspect of God: for in human personality there are not only qualities of spirit and mind, but also a measure of active power such as shows itself in creative energy, or indeed in any activity. Its absence is the sign of the termination of life. An analysis of human life-energy has never been made on the lines of the analysis of matter. But may it not be that the life-energy which creates physical growth and which expresses itself in moving, changing and constructing things may also be analysable into energy patterns of an electronic type. If so, it would, on its small finite scale, be reducible to power of the same type as that which constitutes the material universe: it would then be comparable with, and on its finite scale similar to, the power units or patterns which express themselves in matter. Our life energy expends itself is making physical alterations; and the physical alterations made by us are alterations of the electronic patterns which are fundamentally of the same kind as our own operative energy. Our wills and actions are like those of a swimmer in the sea: he has enough power to displace and move a minute quantity of water by his will to swim and his action as a swimmer, but the main mass and rhythmic movement of the ocean is virtually unaffected. The situation as between our puny life-energy, and the energy of which the material world is composed, is a power of limited activity within the cosmic activity of the Creator. The reduction of matter to energy perhaps supplies the basic explanation not only of God as creator but also of our own limited freedom of activity within his world. 'Earthly power doth then show likest God's.' The error of theologians may have lain in conceiving God as an *aggregate* of spiritual qualities instead of a person; and in conceiving that he can be a person without the physical attribute of energy and power. If we realize God, to some extent analogically, as a Person, and if we remember that active energy is one of the chief characteristics of persons, there is a possibility of understanding him as Creator, and this world as his.

5

INCARNATION

AND IN JESUS CHRIST HIS ONLY SON OUR LORD

HERE we arrive at the vital and central differentia of the Christian religion. It is centred on a fully human and historical person who is also said to be divine. The title Christ claims that he is the Messiah to whose advent the Jews were looking forward. But the Greek word which means 'anointed' savours of adoptionism, as indeed does St. Paul's statement[1] 'concerning his Son who was born of the seed of David according to the flesh, and was defined as son of God in power according to the spirit of holiness in that he rose from the dead'. Son is, of course, not strictly literal but metaphorical. When it was taken literally men asked how one who was fully man could have God as his Father. And the answer given was that of St. Luke in recording the words of Gabriel to Mary: 'The Holy Ghost will come upon you and the power of the Most High will overshadow you and therefore the holy child to be born will be called "Son of God".[2]' However pious and beautiful the story of the virginal conception of Mary may be, to accept it as factually true, apart from the physical crux of a purely spiritual fatherhood, is to deny the perfect humanity of Our Lord. Besides, the genealogies which aimed at showing Jesus to be of the seed of David can only trace this through Joseph as father, and there are suspicious variations in the text. There seems to be no sign in the Gospels that Mary regarded her first-born son as in any way divine, nor is there much trace of Mariolatry in the earliest Church, nor any historical foundation for the immaculate conception of Mary or of her Assumption. These two later doctrines are obviously

[1] Rom. I. 4. [2] Luke I. 35.

consequent on the belief in original sin transmitted from Adam to the subsequent generations by sexual union. The birth of Jesus was a natural birth in an honoured and religious family in a community in which simplicity and piety were virtually uncontaminated. Jesus himself was a boy of a deeply religious temperament: he learned a trade (that of a carpenter) like all Jewish boys, and was well instructed in the Jewish scriptures. There is no reliable record of any superhuman characteristics until the story of his baptism by John. And the attempt of St. Matthew to explain why the Son of God submitted to 'baptism for the remission of sins' is not convincing.[1]

Yet the conviction of the divinity of Our Lord is strong, and ineradicable from Christian minds. It would appear that about the time of his baptism Jesus underwent a unique spiritual experience. He became convinced that God had chosen him and set him apart as the messenger of his kingdom. He offered himself to be God's instrument with complete faith and obedience: he gives himself wholly to God's spirit, and his self offering was met by an outpouring of divine power and insight. He was irradiated, transformed, chosen, and endued with power from on high. He was one with the Father in a way in which no prophet or saint has ever been. 'In him dwelt all the fulness of the Godhead bodily.'[2] In him the complete being of God, by God's own choice, came to dwell. Through him God chose to reconcile the whole world to himself. In the man Jesus Christ the personal being and power of God was completely shown to mankind through a chosen servant, in so far as it could be shown in terms comprehensible to man.

This view might well be called Adoptionist, but is only so in a loose sense; for the Spanish heresy of Elipandus made a distinction between the Logos as true and eternal son of God, and Jesus as an adoptive 'son' metaphorically. As I understand it, the Word or Logos, expressing God's wisdom, will and love became so closely united with the personality of Jesus

[1] Matt. 3. 15.

[2] Col. 2. 9.

that he was 'God-possessed' and rightly realized himself as God's emissary for the proclamation of his Kingdom. He was completely man, but he expressed through his humanity a unique revelation of God—so completely that it is true that 'God was in Christ'. The union of the two natures in Christ was a unity of spirit so complete, a union of the Logos with a human personality, that God spoke through him to the world, and still speaks. Granted that God is personal, his presence in Christ for the manifestation of his glory to man involves none of the desperate efforts of third and fourth-century theologians to explain the unity of the two natures in Christ, whether by a theory of two persons loosely united, or by Apollinarius' partition of the personality, or Arius' creation of a separate though divine person. There is no need for a two-in-one, if Christ in the fulness of his human personality committed himself wholly to God and was received into a union never before or afterwards complete, but capable of partial realization in the most devoted of his followers: St. Paul's doctrine of Christians as in a sense 'in Christ' and their denotation as 'sons of God' express this, as of course does the doctrine of the presence of the Holy Spirit in believers. The impact of Christ on those who knew him was so strong, that almost immediately he became to them Kyrios, Lord. 'Only begotten Son of God' is easily understood (much better indeed than the word begotten is understood) as indicating Christ as the New Man, the first and only man who became fully God-possessed. A dual origin of the two natures as on the one hand 'begotten' from all eternity and on the other as born of Mary is more clearly understood when we realize that God as the eternal wisdom fully expressed himself in Jesus the man who gave himself and was chosen, elect, and received as the Father's instrument and self-revelation.

Does this in any way diminish the glory and uniqueness of Jesus Christ? Belief in God as a person is undiminished. Belief in his revelation of himself through the Son remains. Fatherhood and sonship are conserved, for God is always

Father to Jesus, and Jesus in his obedience and unity of will and God-filled life is all that Son implies. Jesus is forever exalted above mankind by the fulness of the presence of God with him. Jesus as Christ fulfils the Messianic prophecies, and as God-possessed is rightly named as Lord. The Christological debates are seen either as errors caused by trying to add the divine nature to the human nature in one person, or as a solution that ends in the paradox of a God–Man. For all practical purposes this is what he was: but a man chosen and possessed by God, to speak with his voice and live his life on earth, is comprehensible and not illogical, and consistent in the main with the N.T. understanding. There are difficulties still to be considered, notably in connection with the Atonement, and, to a less degree, with the Holy Spirit. But the general picture is persuasive. God was in Christ, Christ was in God. The metaphor 'came down from Heaven', of which the literal interpretation is so difficult, is applicable to the adoption of Jesus by God to be the Herald of his Kingdom and the 'New Man' and the means of his revelation. The unity of Jesus with the Father was so close that he could truly say 'I and the Father are one'.

The researches of Biblical Critics are undermining our assurance that we have accurate pictures of Jesus Christ even in the Synoptic Gospels. We can only restore him historically, as a great Jewish teacher and wonder-worker who was convinced that he was the Messiah of Jewish expectation. But we have further certainties. Firstly that the early Christians came to regard him as divine: secondly that this belief was largely based on a belief in his resurrection: thirdly that this led rapidly to a victorious church interpreting itself and its Master to the world by theologies, most notably those of John and Paul. Fourthly that attempts were made, as soon as the Christian community became a reality, to portray the life and teaching of the Master from any available oral tradition or written sources: fifthly, that in this collection there emerged, together with a number of legends, teaching of such spiritual depth and vitality that it has continued to be the wonder and inspiration of millions.

The summation of these historical certainties points to a supreme religious genius at the very least, and if the Resurrection belief be accepted, to one whose closeness to God passed into a new stage of life after death, which was for a time manifested to certain witnesses, who were so strongly convinced that they proclaimed it everywhere. All this seems to be consistent with what we have previously said of the person of Jesus Christ. As he had conceived himself in terms of Jewish expectations and eschatology and as the first believers in his divinity were Jews, he was set forth to the world primarily as the Creator of a New Israel, foretold by the prophets and transforming the legalism of later Jewry to a new covenant of redemption and faith. On this conception the Christian Church was founded, though it soon absorbed other elements from Graeco-Roman thought and religious ideas. It expressed itself necessarily in an organization of scattered centres of worship into a Church, which guarded continuity by its ministry, unity by its sacraments, and authenticity by its Gospels and 'Apostolic' writings. Those who have seen in this process the guidance of the Holy Spirit seem to have found the true explanation of a most remarkable and spontaneous growth, which, as it grew, assimilated itself to the political conditions and philosophical thought of successive periods. The seed planted by Jesus Christ became a great tree because of its inherent truth and vitality, but soil and climate played their part in its development.

Note to Chapter 5

ADOPTIONISM IN THE NEW TESTAMENT

The voice from Heaven after our Lord's baptism is recorded as 'Thou art my beloved son in whom I am well pleased.' In Matt. 3. 17 and Mark 1. 11 the voice would appear to be part of Christ's vision when he saw the heavens rent open and the Holy Spirit descending in the form of a dove. St. Luke simply says 'It came to pass that . . .' In Luke 3. 22 instead of 'in thee I am well pleased' there is a well-supported v.l. 'This day have I begotten thee.' St. Augustine speaks of this as the reading of some MSS though not the most ancient'. It is clearly an echo of Ps. 2. 7: 'The Lord hath said unto me, "Thou art my son this day have I begotten thee." This psalm is Messianic. St. Paul (Rom. 1. 4) regarded it as fulfilled at the Resurrection when Christ was 'declared to be son of God in power'.

However, the narrative of the voice from heaven and the words 'Thou art my beloved son', are repeated in the account of the Transfiguration. St. Mark here (9. 7) has 'hear him' and is followed by St. Matthew and St. Luke. St. Matthew's text adds 'in whom I am well pleased'. St. Luke has 'my elect son'—ἐκλελέγμενος 'selected' or 'picked out'. In both cases the episode is visionary.

If the record of the voice at Baptism and at Transfiguration is a doublet, to which event shall we assign it? 2 Pet. 1. 17 definitely assigns it to the Transfiguration. If the Transfiguration is to be accepted as a Post-resurrection appearance, St. Paul's reference might be to this in Rom. 1. 4. If this is so his speech in the synagogue at Antioch is apposite (Acts 13. 33). 'God hath fulfilled the promise given by the fathers to us their children, having raised up Jesus, as it is written in the second psalm "Thou art my son, this day have I begotten thee." '

Now it is probable that the author of Hebrews knew the story of the voice; and he believed that it quoted the second psalm exactly. In Heb. 1. 5 we have 'Unto which of the angels said he at any time "Thou art my son: this day have I begotten thee." ' And again in 5. 5: 'So also Christ glorified not himself . . . but he that said unto him "Thou art my son: this day have I begotten thee." Did he refer the voice to the Baptism or the Transfiguration? It seems clear that he did not believe in a miraculous conception. 'It is evident', he says (7. 14), 'that our Lord rose out of the tribe of Judah'. He is the ἀρχηγός, the first of a new kind of glorified manhood. He is (5. 9) 'called of God' and 'made perfect' and 'became' the author of salvation, He 'offered himself without spot to God' (9. 14). He has 'passed into' the heavens (not 'descended from') (4. 14) and 'In the days of his flesh, when he had offered up prayers and supplications, with strong crying and tears unto him that was able to *save him from death* and was heard for his piety [ἀπὸ τῆς εὐλαβείας], though he was son, he learned obedience from what he suffered, and *being perfected* he became to all that obey him cause of eternal salvation, being named by God an high priest after the order of Melchisedec.' This is not the language of a believer in a descended son of God but of an adopted son of man, who entered within the veil as high priest (6. 20) and 'forerunner' for us.

Christ endured the cross 'for the joy that was set before him' (12. 2) and *offered himself* to God through the eternal spirit (9. 14), though himself an elect son of man.

When this is coupled with the absence of any reference to the Nativity it is abundantly clear that the author of Hebrews held adoptionist views.

When we turn to the speeches recorded in Acts, even though they may represent what the author St. Luke believed to have been said, and not verbatim records, we find the same adoptionist views, with a special emphasis on 'the Seed of David' and no reference to a miraculous conception. Thus St. Paul in the synagogue at Antioch (Acts 13. 23) reminds his hearers how God 'gave Saul' . . . 'gave David' and 'of this man's Seed hath God according to his promise, *raised* unto Israel a saviour Jesus, when John had first preached before his coming'. In the same speech (13. 33) St. Paul adds that 'God . . . hath fulfilled' the promise, which he gave to the fathers, to us their children having *raised up* Jesus as it is written in the second psalm (as above). Jesus has not 'come down'. He is 'raised up'.

St. Peter's speech at Pentecost is in the same vein (Acts 2. 22): 'Jesus of Nazareth, a man approved of God among you by miracles, and wonders, and signs which God did by him in the midst of you.' Cf. verse 30 also: 'David . . . being a prophet and knowing that God had sworn to him that of the fruit of his loins he would raise up [one] to sit on his throne.' The The authority for the A.V. reading 'of the fruit of his loins *according to the flesh* he would raise up *Christ* to sit on his throne' is much weaker and suggests dogmatic alteration to interpret the promise of Ps. 132. 11. The use of capitals for 'son', παῖς, here and there in A.V. tends to prejudge the issue as in 3. 13 and 26. In the same speech 3. 22 St. Peter says (from Deut. 18. 15): 'Moses truly said . . . A *prophet* shall the Lord your God raise up unto you of *your brethren* like unto me.' In 3. 25 Abraham's Seed is again emphasized. St. Stephen's speech in 7. 37 uses the same Deuteronomic quotation 'of your brethren'.

St. Peter's sermon at Joppa (10. 38) has also an adoptionist colour; 'How God anointed Jesus of Nazareth with the Holy Ghost and with power.' And St. Paul at Athens (17. 31) speaks of God's judgment of the world 'in a man whom he hath "set apart" or "ordained".'

What then did St. Paul himself believe? He makes no reference to a virginal conception: he is completely sure of the resurrection. By it God has proclaimed Jesus to be the Christ which of course means primarily to St. Paul the Messiah. But his own spiritual experience convinced him that the Messiah conception was not enough. Christ was to be saviour of the world, of Jew and Gentile alike. He was son of God in a special sense, sent 'in the likeness of sinful man' (Rom. 8. 3) to call all men unto his fellowship (1 Cor. 1. 9). He was to manifest the power and wisdom of God

1 Cor. 1. 24). He is the εἰκών of God: God was in him (2 Cor. 4. 4–6). He was 'in the form of God' and 'humbled himself' in order that God might exalt him as Lord above all (Phil. 2. 6–11). The new conception culminates in the magnificent panegyric of Col. 1. 15–20.

And yet, as against all this we have Rom. 8. 29; 'That he might be the first born among many brethren'. In Rom' 1. 3 he is 'declared to be the son of God with power by the resurrection' and in Rom. 5. 17 'the gift of grace which is by one man'. Christ is 'a minister of the circumcision to confirm the promises made to the Fathers' in Rom. 15. 8. In 1 Cor. 15. 20 he is the 'first-fruits of them that slept' (so also v. 23). In the same chapter, verse 21, we have 'by man came also the resurrection from the dead' and 'the last Adam was made a quickening spirit'. In 2 Cor. 5. 21 Christ is 'made to be sin' and in Gal. 3. 13 made a curse. In 2 Cor. 13. 4 'he was crucified through weakness yet liveth by the power of God'. In Gal. 4. 4 Christ is 'made of a woman, made under the law'. In Gal. 4. 14 he is an ἄγγελος or messenger of God. In 1 Thess. 2. 15 the Jews 'killed' him and their own prophets. In Col. 1. 15 he is 'the first born *of every creature*'. In Eph. 2. 5 'God hath quickened us together with Christ' and in 1 Tim. 3. 16 he 'was justified in spirit'. In Gal. 3. 16, 19 and 29 Christ is emphatically 'of Abraham's seed' and in Gal. 4. 31 Christians are said to be children of Abraham through Sarah.

All the above passages seem to have an adoptionist basis, that God selected or empowered the man Jesus to be the Messiah and confirmed that selection by the resurrection in which St. Paul implicitly believed. How can we explain this discrepancy with other passages in which Christ is the divine Lord, sent from heaven, and agent of creation itself? (Col. 1. 15).

The clue may well be in 2 Cor. 5. 16: 'Though we have known Christ after the flesh yet now henceforth know we him no more.' Like many other Christians, St. Paul first believed in Jesus as one pre-eminent in holiness chosen by God to be his Messiah and authenticated as Messiah by the Resurrection. In this he is not unlike the author of Hebrews and the kerygma in Acts. But the problem of how the Messiah could have been crucified and rejected by his own people remained to be faced. The Suffering Servant of God, and the day of Atonement, and the Pascal Sacrifice gave the clue to the cross as a sacrifice for sin. But there was the rejection by his own people of their own Messiah. Then came St. Paul's and St. Peter's calls to the Gentiles. The sin-offering must be somehow a cosmic event, and the law must be superseded by faith, and the Messiah must be somehow a world, and not a Jewish, Saviour.

To St. Paul's mind, and by his mystical experience, a revelation came, as it came to St. John of the Gospel, and to St. John of the Apocalypse and to many of us Christians since, of Christ as Word, of Christ as Son of God, of Christ as world Saviour into whose death Christians are baptised and by whose life they live eternally. 'Thou art my beloved, my elect Son: this day have I begotten thee'. 'Though we have known Christ after the flesh' by our critics, by our historians, by our demythologizers, 'yet now henceforth know we him no more'. The 'voice from heaven' has enlightened us to the reality of God's action in and through Jesus of Nazareth, by whom and in whom he brings salvation to mankind.

6

THE ATONEMENT

JESUS CHRIST was born of the seed of David, brought up in the Jewish religion, taught as an unofficial Rabbi, claiming direct authority of his own derived from his unique relation to God. His mission was to Jews, his disciples were Jews, and so were their first converts. The Apostles did not at first break with Judaism until they were forced out: at the resurrection they realized increasingly the divine in Jesus, and their first conclusion was that in him God had sent the Messiah according to the promise to Israel and Israel's hope. The crucifixion was a grave stumbling block: but there was the resurrection to set against it. And, searching the scriptures they found not only the victorious Messiah sent from Heaven but also the suffering servant. The latter concept, interpreted by Jews as a symbol of their own suffering race, was then seen by Christians as fulfilled in Christ himself. They re-read their scriptures in a new light as the risen Christ had interpreted them to two disciples on the road to Emmaus as 'the things concerning himself'. In the light of this new understanding it became of the highest importance to search the scriptures, and probably a collection or collections of testimonia were gathered which clearly linked the Lord with Old Testament prophecy and prefigurations. These were sufficiently convincing to win over 'many of the priests' to the Messiah–Christ.[1]

This enlightenment connecting Jesus with the old Israel was of course a main aspect of the first Christian preaching, as e.g. in St. Stephen's defence; and it may later have influenced the Gospel writers, St. Matthew in particular, and the manner in which the portrait of Jesus was presented. Among other effects, it brought the sacrificial doctrines and practice of

[1] Acts 6. 7

Judaism into relation with the 'scandal' of the Cross. Its explanation seemed clearly to be found in this. The Cross was the sacrifice of the Paschal Lamb inaugurating a new covenant: as the lamb had sealed the deliverance from Egypt and the adoption of Israel as God's people, so the Cross sealed with the blood of Christ the deliverance from the bondage of sin and the adoption of Christians as a new Israel of God. It was a perfect symbol. The principal motive of Jewish sacrifices had been the restoration of a right relation between the offender and God, and the sacrifice of himself by Christ similarly restored sinners to peace with God. Christ, ascended, became our great High Priest whose self-offering, conceived as cosmic and eternal, once for all, abolishes the old sacrifices which now become unnecessary as they are transcended by the heavenly offering continually renewed in the Eucharist. Thus for Jewish converts the breach with the old religion was healed by the new covenant, and the worship of the God of Israel was conserved. The atonement was fully absorbed into the Jewish 'schema'.

Valuable as this doctrine of atonement was for the transition period, and valuable as it still is for the continuity of the revelations of the Old Testament with those of the new, and for the priestly functions of the Christian ministry, the symbol of the Paschal Lamb was not adequate for the outspreading of Christianity in the Gentile world. The sacrificial doctrine of the Atonement was the product of personal thinking. The human thinker faced the objective fact of the Cross and resurrection against his thought-background of the religion of Yahweh. The fusion of the three elements produced the solution. It was not a theory, a speculation, about the Atonement. It was an understanding of the Atonement in the light of a thought-background, held with firm conviction.

But the primary beliefs of Jewry were not those of the Gentile populations. To look at the Cross and Resurrection in the light of the Jewish sacrificial system was meaningless to them. Under what terms of ultimate reference could it be presented to their minds? To the factual and official mind of Rome the Cross was the execution of a rebel as seen against the thought-background of the Empire, and the resurrection was discounted as a fabrication. But to the Christian, Cross and resurrection were one event and the fact that the risen Christ was no longer to be seen had to be included in its presentation. And its connection with the complex experience of sin and guilt had to be established. From the first, Christians had baptism as an admission ceremony to their brotherhood, and of course the conception of sin as contamination was widespread and instinctive. Admission to a purified society by washing of the stains of sin was a symbol easily understood in the light of the general notion of sin. But it provided no reference to the Cross and resurrection, nor to eternal life. There were, however, prevalent background conceptions popularized by the mystery religions. New life, as well as cleansing, was thought to be obtainable by initiation after purification. Entering into the life of a saviour deity through 'mysteries' was dreamed of. The initiate, as in the religion of Isis, took part in some drama of death and immortality: at Eleusis the rebirth of the Corn-Goddess conveyed to her worshippers a sense of being purified and drawn into communion with an undying life; in Orphism rites of purification and sometimes orgiastic excitement brought moods of ecstasy and glimpses of Elysium; in Mithraism, which was beginning to develop from Zoroastrianism in the first century, the initiate was 'born again into eternity' after a baptism of blood.

In spite of efforts to prove the independence of the development of Christian thought from the mystery religions, there must remain a strong impression that the Pauline presentation of salvation owed something to the floating ideas of his age. We have the initiation by baptism into the death of the Saviour deity, the new life which it promised, salvation through the blood of the Cross, and the assurance of immortality. The new life in Christ was a mystical sharing of the life of the risen and eternal Saviour made possible in Baptism by 'a death unto sin and a new birth unto righteousness'. The spiritual life of the baptized was to be sustained by a communion feast at which the body and blood of Christ were, symbolically at least, 'taken and received' by the participants. This led, of course, to a reinforcement of the Jewish sacrificial idea of the Atonement, by a conception of a mystical union, made possible by Cross and resurrection, with the Saviour. His death atoned for human sin: his resurrection 'brought life and immortality to light' and the gift of his Spirit bound Christians into unity with his eternal being. A new symbolism was inspired and recognized as true.

For Christians it is the fact and not the theories of the Atonement that is paramount The assurance of the forgiveness of sins is a spiritual experience which has recreated countless lives. Belief in it may well have been induced by the ancient sacrificial system and the 'new covenant' among Jewish converts, and by affinities with the ferment of mystical religions among Gentiles; but that was part of the religious climate in which Christianity was born. The experience, apart from reasons for belief, was real, and is real. Explanations of it and justifications of it have notoriously varied from age to age. The Church is committed to the vital truth, and not to its explanations. We may, therefore, reverently seek a presentation of the truth in terms of our own age, without committing ourselves to the manner in which it was understood by former generations. For example the 'satisfaction' theory of Anselm is as dead as feudalism, the Juridical theory of the Reformers is now seen as divisive of the Godhead, as though the love of the son saved from the outraged justice of the Father: the Ransom theory is quite outdated: the 'Christus Victor' theory is analogical; the theory of Vicarious Penitence is untenable since penitence is only possible for a sinner. In various ages the Atonement was understood through various thought backgrounds.

Clearly any explanation must be linked closely with Christology. And the Christology indicated in the previous chapter must be the clue for those who may consider it to be convincing. Its basic idea is revelation—Christ as the man in whom God has definitely revealed himself. That revelation includes: (1) A blaze of divine quality shining on earth, setting before man an ideal of life which is the magnet of those who would be perfect, and their despair. For one aspect of the incarnation is power to show us to ourselves as what we are—sinners, and to create the desire for a purgation of our former ways and a new life. (2) Secondly the incarnation revealed an unbounded love of God for man, a love which did not falter even on the Cross when Christ's enemies had done their worst. This love showed itself in healing and forgiving. It showed its power to cleanse and to recreate; its only condition for this work of salvation was faith in the would-be recipient of the saving power. The Cross itself was not a means of salvation; it was the almost inevitable fate of a perfect life in a sinful world; but its emotional effect in showing the indomitable power of divine love has made it forever a redeeming sign. It awakens man to the realitles of what sin can do and what love can do.

In what sense then is the Cross an Atonement? As Dr. Bezzant pointed out in an article in *Objections to Christian Belief*,[1] it is difficult to see how the physical death of Christ in A.D. 29 can annul the spiritual death of sin today. The conception that all human sin can be loaded on to a cosmic Christ, who gains the power to annihilate it by his human suffering, is fantastic. If it is replied that the suffering on the Cross was more than human we have either patripassionism, rightly rejected by the Church, or an incarnation so total that Christ's enemies were able to crucify physically the divine in him as well as the human: but as we have seen the presence of God in him was spiritual and therefore uncrucifiable. His cry of dereliction shows that in his humanity he suffered the worst of all despairs. If he endured the crucifixion with a guarantee of resurrection he did not die as man dies. His faith in God

[1] P. 94.

had previously given him assurance of eternal life, if his predictions of the resurrection are not, as scholars are inclined to think, inserted *vaticinia ex eventu*. To say that our sins were the cause of his passion is an impossible rejection of the present into the past, unless we are to think of Christ's incarnate suffering as eternal, which would be intolerable, or else to regard sin in a somewhat Pauline sense as a permanent condition into which all humanity is immersed, remedied by a cosmic victory won by Christ. But if the crucifixion was a cosmic act of God it makes a real incarnation unbelievable. Jesus dies on the Cross: but the revelation of God in Jesus could not die.

What then is meant by his 'dying for the sins of the whole world' and how is an atonement effected by the crucifixion? The word ὑπέρ so often used in this connection means 'for', 'on behalf of'; its proper use is as when we say that a soldier died 'for' his country. It does not mean 'instead of' or even 'because of'. Jesus as leader of the apostles died for them, and they escaped. He died to complete his mission to the world, and recognized his end as the Father's will. Such is the plain sense of the synoptic gospels. In St. John we find the mystical conception of the Cosmic Christ whose death was offered 'for the life of the world' (6. 51; 11. 52). In Acts we return to the synoptic sense, in the repeated phrase 'dying for the name' of Jesus Christ. Obviously there is no substitutionary sense here. It is to St. Paul that the substitutionary theory owes its origin, particularly in 1 Cor. 15. 3, 'Christ died for our sins', and Gal. 1. 4; 2. 20; 3. 13. His 'Christ mysticism'—the doctrine of Christians as 'in Christ', baptized into his death, and participating in his risen life—is responsible for a use of the word ὑπέρ which elsewhere he uses normally. From St. Paul onwards this ecclesiological doctrine of the Atonement has prevailed, and yet at the Last Supper it does not appear that Our Lord did more than use the bread and wine as symbols of his approaching self-sacrifice, for there is little doubt that he could have escaped had he wished, and asked them to keep the simple ritual ceremony in his memory.[1] He offered his life for what he knew to be his Father's will, and his Father's purpose in showing himself to the world. Does this lessen our adoration of God in Christ and of God through Christ? Certainly not the adoration; but there is the question of personal commitment. If my sins are forgiven through Christ's death on the Cross, as most Christians at all periods of the Church have believed, a personal debt is felt and a personal communion of love is created. And further, the Church into which we are baptized as token of sharing in his death and resurrection, becomes a community of the redeemed or at least potentially redeemed. Is it possible for an historical and revelationary view of the death and resurrection of Christ to supply the human need of an assurance of forgiveness to the same degree? The Atonement certainly becomes exemplary. It reveals God forgiving and God undying; it reveals a supreme love, faith and obedience. What can that do for one who now feels 'tied and bound with the chain of his sins': who feels 'so fast in prison that he cannot get loose'?

He can certainly conclude that God loves him: he may also realize from Christ's assertion of his power to forgive that it is also possible for him to be forgiven. The forgiveness granted by Jesus was conditional upon faith in him as revelation of God. It is possible for us to have the same faith now and further to believe in his present union with the Father eternally. It is possible for us, further, to believe in his continued presence and influence by his Spirit. And it is therefore possible to ask him for forgiveness, as it was asked and granted *before there was any crucifixion*. He himself said that he had power on earth to forgive sins *before* he was crucified. Belief in God's forgiveness granted through the living Christ can be as real as belief in God's forgiveness granted through the merits of the Crucified One. The faith required is faith in God, and in Christ as the revelation of God, and not in Calvary as a cosmic sacrifice, or oblation, or satisfaction.

[1] See further chapter xi "Holy Communion".

7

THE RESURRECTION

THE evidence for the bodily resurrection of Christ has been studied more minutely than any event of past history: it is admittedly obscure: it is unparalleled; it is susceptible of several interpretations. And yet if it happened, the accounts of such evidence as he gave, in such circumstances, and to such people as he gave them, were bound to be less clear and factual than a scientific historian would desire. It seems to have been God's purpose to leave room for faith. The evidence was given only to those who were already won to allegiance by the incarnate Jesus: it was sporadic: and it came quite unexpectedly. For even if it was foretold, the disciples do not appear to have understood. Its electrical effect is a strong argument that something unprecedented had happened. There is evidently an intention in the Gospels to emphasize that the resurrection was corporeal and not visionary, and yet aspects of the appearances and of angelic presences suggest vision or legend. The problem of the empty tomb is the greatest crux. St. Matthew's account is complicated by the Angel visitor and the command of the risen Lord to meet him in Galilee. St. Mark, so far as he goes, seems to be the source of St. Matthew, who has somewhat embroidered it. St. Luke's story, though he has two angels, is more consistent.

He adds an appearance on the Emmaus road, and to the assembled disciples. St. John is the most explicit: he elaborates the appearance to Mary Magdalene, adds a second appearance to the assembled disciples which results in St. Thomas' confession, and in the twenty-first chapter, if it be his, adds the idyllic story of the appearance by the lake of Galilee.

The Christian belief in the resurrection of the body no doubt originated from the corporeal nature of the recorded appearances: if the resurrection of Christ was 'of the body' there are elements in the story which indicate that his risen body had superhuman powers, and was the same as and yet different from his incarnate body. The belief was not in accordance with those of other religions, for the most part at least, nor with philosophies. But it was firmly held not only by the witnesses, but by sub-Apostolic Christians generally, as, for example, St. Ignatius. There must have been strong grounds on which it was founded. St. Paul tries to solve the crux by his conception of a 'spiritual body'—this self-contradictory idea conserves the continuity of personal life and may have been deduced from the nature of the appearances. It seems, however, to be of a ghostly character, and does not fit some of the appearance stories in which eating, drinking and touching are emphasized. After all a 'body' is not spiritual, and the analogy of the grain of wheat is imperfect for St. Paul's purpose. On the other hand if personal immortality is to be believed, bodily form seems a necessity if only for recognition, and for the belief in the continuity in expression of human personality.

The attempt to explain the resurrection stories as myths based on the disciples' strong sense of Christ's continued presence, or on a feeling that they had been liberated by his life (Van Buren) break down on the facticity of the narration, and the recreative effect of the new belief on the disciples and the early Christians. Such myths, if the product of wishful thinking or imagination, would be less detailed and probably more consistent, and they would not have sent out the Apostles as missionaries of good news for the whole world. Can they then be visions, as it does seem that St. Stephen's and St. Paul's great experience were? As told, they have not a visionary character, except perhaps in the case of the Ascension: and we would have to assume collective visions which present great difficulties. That they are deliberate inventions is impossible in view of the character of those who promulgated them, and the effect which they had. M. Goguel suggests self-projections of Christ 'from the beyond'. This involves a power in his risen spirit of convincing self-materialization, and although one does not care to suggest any limitation of the power of the risen Saviour, one must ask why such self-manifestations should have ceased abruptly. It may have been because the Holy Spirit was to give adequate assurance of the continued life of Christ for all generations after Pentecost.

Visions of the departed have been known frequently, but materializations are questionable. These manifestations between the resurrection and the Ascension would give no assurance about the future to any believer except of the fact that Jesus was living after his death. The suggestion that his death might not have been real, and that he was somehow 'spirited away' and concealed—as in Moore's fantasy *The Brook Cherith*—and Schonfield's *Passover Plot*—is utterly unwarranted by the evidence and unbelievable.

What then remains? If belief in the resurrection of Christ is to be accounted as true historically—there is no difficulty in believing it as true spiritually: namely that the life of God, as seen in the Son of Man, was untouchable by death—if it is to be believed as factual it must give real insight into the nature of immortal life as a possibility for all men. If it happened to one who was perfect man and if, as he taught, his followers are to be made capable of sharing to some degree the destiny of 'Sons of God' any explanation of the resurrection appearances must be in a strong sense continuous with human conditions of life, and give some real intimation of immortality to mankind.

No lesson is more clearly taught in the New Testament and in Christian experience than the creative power of love, and self-sacrifice. The truest love involves a disregard of, and indeed a virtual elimination of the self, in devotion and sacrifice often, and sometimes in adoration. To be loved can recreate character: to know forgiveness as a fruit of love can release from the burden of sins; in loving the lover forgets himself if it is true love, and the love for fellow men has led to countless lives of self-devotion. Love tends always to the elimination of self in experiencing what is loved. Such love is known to scholars, it is felt by lovers of the beautiful in art, poetry and music: it is exemplified in personal love, and in religious devotion. Love is the supreme *creative* power, and it is both felt to be, and revealed, as triumphant over death.

The mystery of death cannot be fully probed: but, as it appears to us, it is the elimination of the individual self as a 'selfish' unit. This does not involve the elimination of persons except in so far as they have lived for self-gratification. Of such selfishness all that can be said apart from the hope of everlasting mercy, an unknown possibility, is that the individual has 'had it'; or as Christ said of pretenders to exceptional veneration 'they have their reward'. *Love seems to confer immortality on that which is truly loved.* The elimination of the self—its passions and desires—does not mean the elimination of the pure and non-selfish experiences of love in which the personality experiences a life which is outside the egoistic graspings, and personal immortality is life in all we have loved. This is at the root of the conviction that love cannot die, any more than the love of Christ could die on the Cross. It is also the foundation of the hope and desire of a future life, which would be meaningless to us as persons if it were not lived in an environment of what we have known and truly loved. The individual self, which is even here obscured and almost lost in loving, would simply not be missed if our true loves here constitute our lives hereafter. This is a necessary anticipation of my later treatment of eternal life, in so far as its nature illuminates faith in the resurrection.

Although the veil of death normally hides the loved departed from our sight, there have been many authentic experiences of lovers who have felt their loved ones present and almost, as it were, recreated in moments of exceptional clarity. Milton's sonnet which begins

> Methought I saw my late espoused saint
> Come to me, like Alcestis, from the grave

might be paralleled in the psychic history of many others.

I am not writing of any attempt to force the barrier through mediums. I mean genuine unexpected materialization in veridical vision or in sense of presence which have brought comfort to many mourners; the spirit of the loved one appears in such cases as he or she was known in this life, and not in any angelic transformation: and the greater the previous love and intimacy the stronger is the impression and the consequent happiness, or sense that all is well.

Now Jesus had been the central focus of the lives of his disciples. They had left all to follow him: they remembered his words more fully and accurately than any man's words have ever been remembered. The love between them and him had been deep, and the intimacy almost unexampled. He had brought them out of themselves into a life dependent on him and complete in self-sacrifice. The desolation when he was torn away was felt by men to whom his every look and tone and word and gesture was intimately known. The preconditions for a momentary restoration to their consciousness of the Jesus whom they had known by their love were perfect. They had a *foretaste of experiences which would be theirs eternally* by seeing and meeting him alive 'after his passion', It was their love for Jesus and his love for his human companions which created for a few brief hours here a foretaste of the eternal conditions in which they would live. It should be noted that the effect of the appearances was not only to bring the conviction that Jesus lived. They created in the disciples' mind a vivid sense of their own eternal life. They were forever 'alive unto God through Jesus Christ'. They had experienced even in this life what they would experience hereafter. The appearances were a foretaste of eternity for those to whom they were vividly possible, namely to those to whom in the flesh Jesus had been the centre of their love. The appearances ceased because they were such that they could only happen to those who had known and loved the incarnate Christ. Their conviction was unshakable: but henceforth the truth could only rest on their testimony, aided by the inspiring power of the

Holy Spirit. Yet even so, it was strong enough to be the germ of the Church. The assurance of the victory of Christ over death was understood in all kinds of ways by early believers. Its root was in the experience of a few to whom brief foretastes of the life hereafter were given because to them only could Jesus, as he was on earth, be part of their eternal life as re-created by love, by mutual love. The Jesus who will be part of the eternal life of Christians generally will be as real as their devotion and imagination have made him, as the Lord and giver of all that they have truly loved in the surround which their loves have created for their eternal happiness, when the self-regarding motions have ceased to activate them, and their loves endure and mutually give them a richer life. When Christ ceased to be incarnate and to have an earthly self in his sacrificial death, the way of love and self-sacrifice was opened to all in such truth that St. Paul can speak of our being dead with Christ, and henceforth alive in him. Thus St. John could proclaim the key of life to be 'love one another', and that 'He who does not love abideth in death':[1] and thus also an insight of existentialism is plausible, namely that we ARE as we appear to other people, though there should have been added 'and to God'.

As I have previously written of the processes of human thought, there are three factors to be taken into account when considering the resurrection stories. There is the experienced fact, the personal situation of the experiencer, and the thought background from which he has the experience. We know the situation of the witnesses, bereaved and suddenly over-joyed: we have seen what appears to be the character of the appearances, a recreation by mutual love of a loved presence: the thought background of the disciples was essentially that of their day—a three-story universe, a belief in spirits, beneficent or malevolent, an expectation of a Messiah from heaven, a transcendent God, and a possibility of miracles. There is little doubt that this thought-background coloured their reports

[1] 1 John 3. 14.

of the appearances, but it is not possible to estimate the extent of this third factor. Their conclusion, however, was definite—that the Jesus they had known and loved had met with them, talked with them, and even eaten with them after his death and burial.

8

THE HOLY GHOST

IN treating the doctrine of the Holy Trinity something has already been said on the nature of belief in the Holy Ghost, the third Person of the Trinity. It was a long time before he was realized as a third Person of the Godhead and in the creed of Nicea the bare statement of belief in the Holy Spirit was considered adequate. The personality of the Holy Ghost seems to be realized in the Acts of the Apostles as an active source of inspiration and guidance of a kind which could not be ascribed to the glorified Christ. And yet in the Epistles of St. Paul the spirit of Jesus and the Holy Spirit are sometimes synonymous. St. John's Gospel is the main authority for a separate personality, but his theology is generally recognized as a theology of a mystical type, a presentation according to John, which in these days must be understood as one of a number of facets of the divine life presented by the New Testament. If God is Spirit and Person it is most difficult to conceive of him as divided, rather than as one divine spirit known in three active manifestations.

The Church is rightly said to be the area of the special operation of the Holy Spirit: it is, or should be, a spirit-inspired organism. But the Church is centred on Jesus Christ whose corporate manifestation in human society it is said to be: as such it is inspired by his spirit and intended to prolong the work of his incarnation. It is impossible to make a distinction between the Holy Spirit as the Church's inspiration and the Spirit of our Lord which is equally so. St. Augustine's idea of the Holy Ghost as the bond of union between Father and Son is impossible, as it depersonalizes the Holy Ghost and makes him a relation, and makes the Godhead a Binity and not a Trinity. It is sometimes argued that since love is a fundamental quality of God, and since before Creation God was alone in his Triune Majesty there must be a plurality in the Godhead to make the love-relation possible. This might be so if Father, Son and Holy Ghost are separate persons in the ordinary sense of the word. If their activities are all those of one Personal Spirit and we need not believe in three Persons there is no difficulty about eternal love as being the chief of God's qualities in so far as they are made known to us. The rich hymnology of the Holy Spirit, and the numerous prayers to him, need no alteration if they are addressed to God as Holy Spirit instead of to God the Holy Spirit.

There is one aspect which causes difficulty to those who hold to the coequal and separate person. In some instances the Holy Spirit is spoken of as if he were a gift to the Church and particularly to the ministry by the laying on of hands. This may also apply to Baptism, Confirmation and Unction. The conception is that the *power* of God the Holy Spirit is conveyed from one who has already received it by the imposition of his hands to the other person: the act is conceived as sacramental and not as merely symbolic but it is always accompanied by prayer as implying that the gift is primarily from God. Still the idea of transmission from one to another remains, and only a previously ordained minister, it is said, and particularly the Bishop can convey the gift. The Deacons were so commissioned (Acts 6): so were St. Barnabas and Saul for the Gentile mission (Acts 13. 1–3). Apart from those references in the Acts, the other authorities are in the non-Pauline letters to St. Timothy (1 Tim. 4. 14; 5. 22; 2 Tim. 1. 6), and it is noteworthy that St. Matthias seems to have been elected to the Apostolate after prayer and the casting of lots. The practice of conveying blessing by the laying on of hands has of course Old Testament authority, though anointing was the symbol of ordination. Num. 11. 17 speaks of a transferring of the Spirit which was in Moses to the seventy elders: but it is an act of God and not by laying on of hands. Isaac blessed his sons by a laying on of hands in Gen. Ch. 48. In Acts 8. 17 the giving of the Holy Spirit to Samaritan converts immediately follows the laying on of the Apostles' hands, and in Acts 19. 6 the gift also comes by the laying on of St. Paul's hands. Acts 13. 3 and 4 seems to indicate a similar ordination of St. Paul and St. Barnabas for the Gentile Mission, and 1 Tim. 4. 14 is good evidence, though perhaps late, for the same ordination rite. In Acts 14. 23 and 2 Cor. 8. 19 Χειροτονεῖν seems more probably to refer to election by show of hands which is its regular use in classical Greek. The practice of laying on of hands became traditional in the Church for Ordination, Confirmation, Baptisms sometimes and Unction. Whether it has been a means or channel of the gift of the Holy Spirit, or a symbol of the gift has of course been disputed. To think of it as a means of channelling the grace of Holy Orders in a continuous line of succession implies a doctrine of the Church as sole repository of the authentic gift which unduly narrows the divine action and is belied by marked spiritual gifts in many who have not been so set apart. A symbolic use of the rite is most natural, and adequate to explain the scriptural references and the growth of a *post hoc ergo propter hoc* interpretation. The use of a symbol with strong spiritual intention seems an adequate theory of the laying on of hands as an outward and visible sign of a grace given but not of a Person given. Whatever views may be held on this point, it has an adverse bearing on belief in the separate personality of the Holy Ghost. Sacramental practice would rather point to belief in him as a power than as a person.

Writing about A.D. 380 St. Gregory of Nazianzus speaks of confusion in the Church on the doctrine of the Holy Spirit as follows: (*Orat. Theol.* 5. 8): 'Of the wise men among us some considered the Spirit as an activity, some as a creature, some as God: and some have not known which of these opinions to choose, in reverence, as they say, for Scripture, as if it made no clear declaration.' Neither it does. Dr. Leonard Hodgson[1] admits that New Testament authority is divided

[1] *Doctrine of the Trinity*, pp. 80–4.

between 'he' and 'it' passages, but his reasons for accepting the 'he' passages as more authentic are not convincing. His acceptance of the orthodox view leads him to a conception of an organic type of Trinity as possessing unity in an 'internally constitutive sense'[1]. He fails to make it clear what kind of unity can possibly make three personal centres of activity describable as one. He postulates, without proving, a new kind of unity beyond the mathematical and beyond the organic, and attributes it to God on the sole grounds of Christian experience.

The immense theological efforts of the Church in the first four centuries to combine three full and equal personal realities in one Godhead produced not only the rejection of Arian, Dynamic and Modalist heresies, but also a division in the concept of substance in support of orthodoxy. Granting that there must be one underlying divine substance, theologians were faced with the problem of how it would be said that 'the Father is God, the Son is God and the Holy Ghost is God, and yet there are not three Gods but one God'. It was strangely solved by separating the substance predicable of the Godhead in general from the substantial reality which must be ascribed to each person. For the latter they used the term 'hypostasis' and made it mean 'that which constitutes and unifies a centre of personal reality'. And thus it could be said that one divine reality underlay its three hypostases or personal manifestations. But a new difficulty arose. The οὐσία of Godhead was not susceptible of division and therefore must exist in its fulness in each of the three hypostases. It followed that in each hypostasis the qualities of Godhead must be fully present even if not always active. Hence came the doctrine of περιχώρησις or *circuminsessio*, namely that there is interpenetration of the qualities of Godhead between the three hypostases, of each of whom all divine qualities may be predicated. And this produced yet another crux. How then were the Persons to be distinguished? The solution was that

[1] 'Doctrine of the Trinity' p. 107, 8.

the only difference between them lay in that the Father is 'fount of being', the Son has 'begottenness' and the Holy Ghost 'spiration'. And even the term 'begotten' had to be explained as 'eternally generated'—whatever that insight of Origen may mean.

So *omnia abeunt in mysterium*! Of course there must be mystery concerning the nature of God. But not necessarily on irrational rather than supra-rational lines. It is not solved by theories of the Economic, Essential, Psychological or Organic type. The concept of static substance bedevilled it. If only it would have been realized in terms of life, a divine life manifested to us in three personal modes how much more credible it could be!

9

THE CHURCH

ONE, holy, Catholic, and Apostolic—such are the characteristics of the Church as dogmatically described. Its unity is so far only invisible and scarcely that; but it is being earnestly sought. Its holiness is an ideal imperfectly realized; its catholicity is potential rather than actual. Its Apostolicity is historical and only minimally doctrinal. So what is being described? Is it an ideal still unrealized, a 'project' of the Church, as existentialists would say, a teleological society, or is it the 'form' or 'idea' of the Church of Christ, on Platonic lines, i.e. the church as it really is in its essential being, imitated on earth by imperfect copies? This seems plausible. Or is it an invisible church of those whose hearts are in true allegiance to the Saviour, and who are a scattered elect among all 'churches'? It seems not, because the very word ecclesia implies a visible society at work in the world. Is it a human society or a number of societies of Christian believers formed for the practice and propagation of their faith? It would seem not, because the churches claim to be channels through which divine influence operates in the world. Is it then an organism created by the inner life of the Holy Spirit by means of which those who are sharers in the life of Christ by baptism are spiritually sustained, and through which his will is done in the world? This might well describe a united church, though it would scarcely justify its complicated organization and involvements in society. Is it an ecclesia or assembly of the faithful called out from the world: it was like that at the beginning, perhaps, but its hierarchical and corporate continuity have institutionalized what was primatively simple. As a concept the Church defies definition: in its historical variations and ramifications it defies description: in its sociological aspect it defies classification: and in its influence it defies estimation. The Church means so much to so many people that one ought to be able to say what it is; but their attitudes to it are so divergent that an attempt to define the plain and natural use of the term would defeat any linguistic philosopher. Of course the attempt has been made. 'The visible church of Christ is a congregation of faithful men' says the Nineteenth article of the Church of England 'in the which the pure word of God is preached and the sacraments be duly ministered according to Christ's ordinance in all those things that of necessity are requisite to the same.' Apart from the obscurity of the last phrase, this is only a description of one church, the Church of England as it was in the sixteenth and seventeenth centuries. And it omits as much as it includes, for example the Holy Spirit, the Bible and the Ministry.

Some have defined the Church briefly as the 'Mystical Body of Christ'. But in spite of Papal authority for the phrase the term 'mystical' and Body do not mix. Body means 'corporal expression' and mystical means 'realized spiritually'. If he had said 'Body of Christ in a mystical sense' it might mean that the spiritual presence of Christ still makes himself known on earth through an organic unity of his followers: but it would have to be added that this organic unity of Christians who are spiritually 'in Christ' makes itself apparent in the world through an institutional organization. There is a mediation of Christ through Christians to the world: but it has a twofold character. The individual Christian tries to live after the manner of Christ who sustains his spiritual life: but Christians corporately, knowing their individual weaknesses, try to realize an organic unity as a means of mutual realization of the divine power, especially through the sacraments and preaching of the 'Word'. Such a visible society would become loose without organization. Religions seem normally to have required priests to co-ordinate their worship. In the case of Christianity it was realized that the task of understanding the word and ministering the sacraments required more authority than could be conferred by appointment: it required such a measure of inspiration, dedication and learning as could only be required from those whose lives had been devoted to their task. Christ had ordained the Apostles and according to St. John had given them special spiritual power for this task. The Apostles had ordained others with a similar faith in the conveyance of a special gift. And the Church continued the practice which was not only spiritually requisite but also necessary for organizational stability. So theoretically and to a reasonable extent in practice the Church exists to continue the work of her incarnate Lord as a means for the operation of his spirit, the transmission of his teaching, the mutual help and corporate influence of his followers, and the upholding of obedience to his will which is the will of God. Such is its world-ward aspect. Towards God it offers corporate worship and thanksgiving: from God it mediates love, power and forgiveness. From his spirit it receives constant inspiration by which social life is sustained, and its development influenced: by which also thought is guided and progressive understanding promised. It endeavours to be a light in the world kindled from the Light of the World, and a saviour in the world fulfilling the task of the Saviour of the World. Its character is introvert towards God and extrovert towards God's world, but never adequate for its task of the continual re-presentation of Christ because of the imperfections of its members both individually and corporately. From God the Church is Holy, 'coming down from above'; towards God the visible Church aspires imperfectly, and its mission to the world is dimmed by human weaknesses.

As we review our doctrine of the Church through the mentality of the world of today we must now ask what, if any, modifications are necessary. Many voices are now raised to answer this question. The church is said to be an anachronism, necessary perhaps in the past, but obsolescent now. It is said by Professor MacKinnon to be repressive of intellectually radical ideas, in its triumphalism and ceremonial masquerade to distort the manner and substance of apostolic presence, and, he implies, wedded to an outworn structure of belief. His first charge does not appear to apply to the Church of England of today in which liberty of opinion seem to have been allowed to run wild. I personally would emphatically agree that the ceremonial masquerade is overdone, and in spite of its defenders' contention that it enhances the glory of God, would desire drastic simplification. Some doctrinal reformulation is essential: otherwise this book would not have been written. Yet restatement must be restatement of those perennial truths which are the core of the Church's message to the world.

Extremists would consider an institutional church unnecessary. The world it is said is God's temple and Christians are there who claim it for God by living in it 'in Christ'. As against this, other churchmen contend that living in Christ is really living in the Church which is his body into which we are baptized and in which we are sacramentally sustained. Here the Protestant–Catholic antithesis appears in its sharpest form. The Church of Rome, the strongest of the Churches, is making vigorous efforts to draw other Churches into its unity, believing them to be of value in proportion to their dynamic for reunion. Differences of doctrine are, for the time being, soft-pedalled, not because Roman dogmatic beliefs are changing, but because of the obstacles which they present. There is an increasing drawing together of non-Roman Catholic churches in the Ecumenical movement: here again doctrinal differences, which are not so great, are glossed over. In both cases the minimizing of the importance of doctrine might well be disastrous. For the Church exists to proclaim certain truths to the world: and will never gain allegiance from those who do not believe her proclamation. Sincerity in belief is vital to true religion. Even those who become Christian for other reasons and other impulses do so in the faith that the belief which unites a Church is held sincerely and validated intellectually by its leaders or government. There is no means of universal evangelism except the *ultima ratio* of truth. And the unity of truth in a corporate entity like a Church is such that what might seem minor falsities cannot be tolerated, if they are really false. Faith may reasonably be asked by a Church in what is beyond the power of reason, provided it is not contrary to reason. But once reason has pronounced a belief to be untrue, the insincerity of accepting it spreads over the whole confessional set-up, because truth of coherence is essential to any intellectual *Weltanschauung*. An institutional church from this point of view is a necessary expression of coherence of belief in a number of persons. Differences of doctrine have always been the raison d'être of separated Churches. Their elimination or agreed ambivalence is a prime requisite for reunion. But of course there are many other reasons for institutionalism. Our Lord promised his presence where two or three are gathered together in his name: this implies that the power of the Lord of Life can be more strongly felt when even a few are united in their approach to him. His presence in the Eucharist is also essentially a presence in a gathering of the faithful at a ritual meal. His prayer for unity 'that they may be one even as we are one' implies a gathering of many into unity in him. His gift of the Holy Spirit was made to the Apostles corporately. St. Paul's teaching that Christians are 'the body of Christ and members in particular' implies that they must have a corporate as well as an individual entity. Why? An obvious answer is (1) that Christians share a common spiritual approach to God, and receive common spiritual gifts from God and (2) that Christians acting for God in the world gain strength from their corporate unity, and that those who are not Christian may have a clear knowledge of what, of whom, and where this religion called Christianity is. It must be a city set on a hill if it is to be seen by the world.

Further, if further proof of the necessity of an institutional Church be needed, the essential brotherhood of Christians in Christ must have its corporate expression, and a worship centre and power house from which they operate. Being engaged, for the most part, in activities which are practical and absorb their energies, the body must have a ministry whose main concern is to lead their corporate worship, to study and expound the revelation with which the Church has been entrusted, and to care for the spiritual and temporal needs of those who require such ministry. The Church's warfare against evil needs leaders, and the Holy Spirit in the Church needs interpreters, and society in general needs a tangible expression of the visible aspects of Christ's continuing ministering to mankind.

Thought about the Church, in the Anglican communion as in other Churches is a striking case of personal thinking: I, the thinker, think about the Church through my perspective. This perspective has been formed through my experience of life in the Church of England, through my knowledge of Church history, and my acquaintance with other social institutions. I cannot go back in thought to the apostolic age and begin de novo: too much has happened in between, and gives me a perspective through which I must look. Drastic innovators, in ignoring this perspective and trying to start afresh, break not only with history but with the ways of their own communion; the result is that they cannot carry either their fellow-churchmen or their existing church with them in their ideas; all they can do is ventilate them in books. Reform must be realist, i.e. must take account of the perspective from which it is proposed.

Therefore in suggesting any reconstruction in the Anglican doctrine of the Church, the Church as it is, and has been, and will be, must be visualized, and any change in our conception of it must be such as would carry the consent of thinking churchmen. The essential, though Platonic, idea of the Church as One, Holy, Catholic and Apostolic must be retained. Bible, Creed, Sacraments and Ministry must also be pillars of its edifice. Local affiliations and church buildings must remain, perhaps with modifications. But there are modifications of the concept which seem to be required.

The Church is not truly the Church of England, but the

Church of Christ in England: recognition of this would tend towards reunion, and loosen such affiliations with the state as are hampering to our mission, and this does not include all affiliations. Unity of Church and nation is now an impossible and undesirable part of the conception of the Church.

As to the conception of the Church as bound to a propositional creed which it continually recites and to which it requires general assent there is the difficulty that this inhibits reconstruction of doctrine when no agreement on credal expression of the universal Church could now be reached, and no full acceptance of all the present articles of belief can be demanded of individual members. The Creeds have been hallowed by centuries of use, and have provided a kind of steel framework round which the Church has been built; it is rusty and yet cannot be renewed without taking down the building. It might be sung by a choir or read by an official with some such preface as 'The Catholic Faith is this: we believe, etc.' Or another formulation might even be devised such as 'I believe in God, Father, Son and Holy Spirit, maker and Lord of heaven and earth. And in Jesus Christ as Lord and revelation of God to mankind, who was truly man and truly God; he was crucified for us under Pontius Pilate; he rose from the dead, he liveth eternally, he will be our judge. And in the Holy Spirit who is God with us, and who continually abides in his holy Catholic Church. And in the communion of souls in Christ both living and departed, the forgiveness of sins, and eternal life after death.'

It would also, I suggest, be desirable that the concept of earthly majesty and glory should be dissociated from the ministry of the Church Militant, in so far as it invests individuals. This was a heritage from Imperial Rome and produces pageantry rather than the glory which rightly belongs to expressions of worship. The historic ministry must of course be included in the concept of the Church, but what has been called the 'baronial accretions of the Episcopate' should go. De jure representation in the House of Lords should cease, though political reform will probably include in an upper chamber some eminent churchmen. The one really large scale alteration in the Church of the future should be a drastic pruning of machinery, a purge of unnecessary social activities, and a scrapping of societies for this and that in favour of active participation by individual Christians in state welfare services and local government. The Parish is an essential of the concept of the Church, and its local pastoral ministry to people in their homes should take precedence over attempts to infiltrate elsewhere. Intellectual qualifications and mature age should not bar the way to ordination for those who are 'truly called' and the decision of their fitness should rest with the bishops whose obligation it is to find suitable men through their clergy, and to staff their dioceses. More bishops are urgently needed, and fewer committees. These controversial suggestions are only consequential to an attempt to refurbish the image of the Church for an age in which it has become tarnished by association with peripheral and unnecessary activities.

A principal reason for the present assault on the institutional Church is its identification in the popular mind with moral rigidity, and particularly with a severe code of sexual morality. As a first principle it should be taken that the Church exists to mediate God's love and forgiveness to all mankind. The method of Christ was to change the emphasis from outward observance to inward purity of motive, from law to love. His aim was to change hearts in such a way that an inward spirit of holiness would transform all moral behaviour. Faith hope and love were to transcend the ethical virtues, because their inward presence would necessarily lead to an ethic far superior to any that could be produced by law and casuistry. It was a dangerous line to replace the Jewish commandments and Jewish legalism by 'Love God' and 'Love thy neighbour', but it showed an infinite trust in man. Apart from some general and guiding principles it must be recognized that every moral decision is unique because of the infinite varieties of persons and circumstances. Therefore it is principles and not laws that are required. These involve a free moral agent in responsible personal decision on each occasion of doubt. The principle is as it were our major premise in such reasoning. The 'middle term' is our particular case. But to establish a valid minor premise is our problem. For example: 'X is contrary to the divine law or will.' 'My contemplated act is a case of X.' 'Therefore it would be wrong to do it.' But is my act a case of X? All the circumstances of the act must be taken into account, and the nature of X must be fully understood. One might instance the seventh commandment. When it was given it was conceived mainly as an attack on the most precious possession of any man, i.e., his wife or wives. The love between them was a less prominent factor. A wife has now ceased to be regarded as property except in some legal senses. Love and parenthood have now become the chief constituent of marriage. If the love has ceased and parenthood has not occurred the situation is not the same. The 'law' would not have the same force. But Christ shifted the emphasis towards a view of adultery as a violation of a love-bond, sanctified by marriage. It is not easily believable, especially because of a textual discrepancy, that he legislated here, for the only time. In his teaching love and honour in matrimony become the paramount factors. So it can be seen how very complicated the situation has become, and how wrong it is to outlaw a divorced person from communion with fellow-Christians regardless of the circumstances of the divorce. As to remarriage there are certainly cases in which it seems right under the principle of love and compassion.

Similar perplexities arise under the law against theft in our present social complexity. It is plain enough in the case of personal theft of another's property. But a highly competitive society is one in which a kind of theft is always occurring, such as for example the effort to gain customers who may be buying elsewhere, or to gain an appointment for which, for all we know, a rival may be more suitable, or legalized theft by the State as in death duties or capital gains, or to some extent in betting and gambling. Even the desire to act only in accordance with the law of love may be difficult to apply. Casuistry may attempt solutions, but the principal guide is the individual conscience, and consciences vary enormously because of defective teaching or environment. The solution of moral problems depends, in all but obvious cases when human judgment is adequate, on the guidance of the Holy Spirit, either from personal commitment or from the Church as his social expression. But the Church's interpretation is too often marred by legalism, and inadequately charitable.

10

SOTERIOLOGY

THE Church exists by God's will 'for us men and for our salvation'. It perpetuates the saving work of Christ. But the question 'salvation from what?' immediately arises. 'Modern man' as he appears to some exponents of new theologies does not feel that he needs to be saved: he relies for his well-being on the state, education and technology; his ills can be attended to physically by medicine, emotionally by psychotherapy, and economically by 'relief'. He can find out nothing certain as to the possibility of a future life, and dismisses fears of punishment and hopes of beatitude in it as problematical in the extreme. He has faith in himself, in science, in money and in luck, a good deal of hope that all will be well, and a measure of love for his neighbour. God has ceased to be the centre of his faith, hope and love: and the cardinal virtues are quite adequate as moral aims.

But this picture only applies to the satisfied humanist as he is conceived under the heading 'modern man'. It describes large numbers of people in progressive states, but, even in them, excludes larger numbers of afflicted, lonely, neurotic and underprivileged people. And in overpopulated and semi-civilized countries it applies to comparatively few. The Christian revelation came to a world in which conquest, slavery and barbarism had created a far wider consciousness of need, and the absence of humanistic hope and achievement made its message of 'salvation' a light in a great darkness. People were far more ready to respond because there was no alternative hope in human progress and achievements, and widespread superstition.

To such, salvation meant freedom from many fears and oppressions, hope for a glorious future, overthrow of wickedness, and a new fellowship of love. But what does it mean for today and particularly for the advanced societies? We know where to go for our various needs, where relief, or healing, or advice is obtainable; we have adequate means, and not excessive labour, and a large measure of personal freedom: pleasures are readily available, both the higher and the lower, and friendship is general. One might ask whether the salvation message is only applicable to the unfortunate and suffering minority. They are at present the chief care of a depleted ministry.

Christ, we proclaim as saviour of the world—from what is he saviour? His own words give an answer, or rather two answers—he came to save from sin[1] and from lostness.[2] There is no doubt that sin is a permanent characteristic of human nature. Its cure is repentance. Christ came to call sinners to repentance. Repentance is caused, not by consequences, like remorse, but by recognition of having failed or having done wrong. Even if the Christian denotation of offence against God is not accepted, and the word sin is consequently disliked, no one fails to recognize wrongdoing in himself and others, and wickedness in various degrees, and errors, and failures, and omissions of duty which bring such evil consequences. Christ's way of bringing men to repentance was primarily the example of his sinless life supported by authoritative denunciation, and teaching which opened men's eyes: he did not refrain from using fear, and he proclaimed a coming kingdom of righteousness. Often too he did it by awakening love. His God-filled personality gave immense power to his preaching. This way has been faithfully followed by the Christian ministry.

But to bring to repentance is not to save. Though the sins may be disowned and forsaken the facts remain and the remorse. Temptations and new failures recur. The essence of the saving work of Christ is the pronouncement of forgiveness with all the authority of God, and the renewal of souls by new spiritual strength, by the Holy Spirit. There lies the complete remedy, the 'salvation' from sin. And it is a remedy which no psychoanalyst or rehabilitation can supply to a troubled con-

[1] Mark I. 15. [2] Luke 19. 10.

science. Repentance, absolution and the power of the Holy Spirit are the complete answer to sin, the answer made possible by Jesus Christ. It is needed today as much as ever, even if the need is not always realized.

Secondly Christ proclaimed his mission as to those who are lost. A full realization of this 'lostness' of our contemporaries is made possible by reading existentialist writings. But it is not hard to sense it in ordinary experience, particularly among the young. The purposelessness of life, the constant threat of suicidal wars, the cynicism of politics, the absence of meaning in the 'rat-race', the follies of fashion, the universal money-chase, and the crowded competitive strain of life have produced a sense of futility, nervous disorders and suicides among those who try to think, and in others, who fear to do so, a need of constant diversion and occupiedness.

Being lost has a double sense, not knowing where you are, and not knowing how to go where you desire to be. The first is intellectual lostness and the second moral lostness. Intellectual lostness is common in those who have lost faith, and are dazed by uncertainties of the purpose and ends of life, puzzled by conflicting theories, and without hope of understanding. They turn normally to what they *can* understand, the realities and satisfactions of natural life; they think that after all they didn't ask to be born, that they are sure of certain instincts which can usually be gratified, and cease to worry, usually, about what fate or chance may bring.

Moral lostness involves the character. People who feel morally lost know pretty well what they ought to be, and to do, but after repeated failures they have not enough strength to achieve it. The ideal becomes for them the unattainable: they are distracted by cares, by economic necessities, by lusts and by pleasures. The moral urge only makes them uncomfortable, and good purposes become indefinite and fade out of possibility.

Christians know that Christ's claim to be the way, the truth, and the life is the answer to intellectual lostness, and that the power of the Holy Spirit is the answer to moral lostness. But they may not be equally sure how, precisely, salvation from lostness works, as distinct from salvation from sin.

Intellectual lostness needs firm conviction of truth, knowledge of where precisely we are. Philosophies are highly conflicting and empirical knowledge is not enough. The answer normally given is that one must have faith: that the life of Christian obedience will clear the uncertainties—'He that doeth the will shall know of the doctrine.' To those who say that they cannot achieve faith it is replied that faith is not an achievement, but the gift of God. They should pray for it. This reply savours of obscurantism, and suggests an Augustinian error of God's selecting those to whom he will give faith. Gifts of God are innate in human personality and are generally given, though unequally exploited. A natural tendency to trustfulness in God can be developed and is rewarded by a fading of doubts in many cases. But there are those whose mental development is such that they cannot be satisfied by the childlike trust which Christ commanded. For them the answer can only be such an exposition of Christian theology as can satisfy their minds, and this answer is being gradually worked out by philosophical theologians in spite of divergence of schools of thought—or perhaps because of it—dialectically. There is such a thing as faith in reason to understand the truth, and it is becoming justified increasingly. Salvation by revelation and reason is Christ's way with the intellectually lost.

As to the morally lost—and of course by this one does not mean those who have abandoned themselves to depravity, but those whose lostness is due to moral weakness of character and purpose—God's answer is the power of the Holy Spirit. This is not a magical gift, but the spiritual strength which comes from willed obedience to God's guidance for living. It comes from worship, from self-sacrifice, from devotion to the cardinal virtues, and from openness in faith to hope and love. It can be felt by anyone who resists and overcomes his dominant temptations, and by anyone who seeks it earnestly in worship. The Saviour of the world is still seeking, and still saving from sin and from lostness: his church collectively and his people individually are his instruments. He saves by love, by fear, by illumination, by forgiveness, by power of the Holy Spirit and by truth. His divine power to save shone out from the very powerlessness which he accepted in his incarnate life, and, most of all, from the climax of his Cross, when from utter helplessness and human defeat there sprang the world-moving victory over sin and death.

But, it will still be asked, in what sense did he conquer sin and death? As to sin, its power and reality still remain. It is only conquered in those who receive forgiveness: and only if they sin no more could it be a permanent conquest. It was not conquered, so far as we know, in those who brought Christ to the Cross. But it seems to have been conquered in the penitent thief, who, however, could sin no more. We do not even know that it was conquered in the case of the executing soldiers for whom Christ prayed.

And yet the Christian experience of forgiveness is very real. In Dr. H. R. McIntosh's great book *The Christian Experience of Forgiveness* the answer to the question 'how are our sins forgiven?' is simply that we are dealing with a Personal God whose great love forgives and by forgiveness restores to communion. To forgive is essentially a personal act, and the universal possibility of forgiveness requires an Almighty and Personal God. I cannot see how we can go beyond this in explaining the modality, the 'how' of forgiveness After all, can we explain how any person fully and freely forgives another: except by love, which is our explanation of divine forgiveness also. The teaching of the Lord's prayer seems to indicate that the divine forgiveness depends on the sinner's own forgivingness, as well as in divine love. In the parable of the unmerciful servant his forgiveness is withdrawn because he is not himself forgiving By being forgiving ourselves we, as it were, prepare the ground for the divine forgiveness. Because, it seems, we act as God acts, God himself acts on us similarly. This would make it appear that as God becomes the centre of our active living, our natural and unforgiving self becomes sublimated, and as St. Paul says 'Not I but Christ liveth in me.' If the natural human personality is opened up to God by faith, the divine attitude of God to sinners becomes increasingly our attitude.

11

SACRAMENTS

A RELIGION is not a philosophy. The adherent of a particular philosophy professes his belief in its tenets as an intellectual system, and in so far as they involve action feels an obligation to translate his beliefs into practice. Thus in the past a Stoic would have felt bound to meet misfortune with fortitude, and in the present a Marxist would have to put the interests of the communist party before private obligations. Of what nature is this philosophical obligation? It appears to depend on a sense of integrity which demands that belief and action should be consistent. This sense, in its turn, depends on an inner conviction of the wholeness of mind and body, such as made Euripides' famous line 'My tongue has sworn it, but my mind is unsworn', a scandal to the Greeks. In itself it is an extension into practice of the logical consistency which marks a philosophical system. It is an intellectual compulsion consequent on belief. The body is conceived as that by which the mind can express itself.

In so far as the Christian religion is an expression of intellectual belief the same condition holds. The belief in God involves obedience to his will in so far as it can be known. The belief in God's forgiveness of sins coupled with his known will that we should treat others as we would wish to be treated by them involves in practice forgivingness. The area of moral action enjoined by Christian belief is considerably wider than that imposed by most philosophies because righteousness is believed by Christians to be required of man by God. The belief that God is a judge with power to enforce his sentences is not purely intellectual: it is a belief that such is in fact the case. Whatever righteousness may be caused by this is intellectually caused by assent and emotionally by hope or fear. This belief is only partially intellectual, and virtuous action on such a premise is not solely due to an intellectual compulsion demanding integrity, but also to common-sense assent actuated by hope or fear. Christianity depends not only on intellectual belief but on a claim that it states how things are without much empirical evidence. It is a *Weltanschauung* rather than a philosophy, because of its dependence on revelation.

Being such, its endeavour is to bring human behaviour into conformity with the realities which it proclaims to be the case. Its aim is to induce the adoption of a way of life because it is the best, and in conformity with how things really are. Intellectual grounds may be adduced by philosophical theology to reinforce its proclamation. Its tenets may be shown to be a reasonable scheme of things. But even if assent be given to these, they still demand a more righteous and a more unselfish standard of behaviour than is normal for natural man. True, this demand is reinforced by promises as well as by fears; and the hope of happiness in a future life is a strong inducement. Yet assent and fears and hopes are not in themselves strong enough to overcome the strong natural egoistic instincts and to sustain a life at the level which Christ revealed as possible or even requisite in his followers. His own communion with the Father was the strength of his complete obedience, and his resultant spiritual life and power. His union with the Father was spiritually complete, and two aspects of this which were revealed in his life gave a clue to possibilities for his followers. In his parables he infused the common things of life with spiritual meaning; in his miracles he cured bodily ailments by spiritual power. His cures were normally not by a fiat but by eliciting the co-operation of faith from the sufferer. The opening of the personality by faith in him enabled the power to be effective.

Because all creation is God's it has a spiritual *unterbau* as well as a material expression. The divine 'Word' that brought it into being expressed the divine intention which still lingers in created things, and can be evoked by insight or by faith. The universe in itself is not sacramental but can become sacramental here and there when human spirits realize it, and need it, and treat it so by faith. In such a case 'sacramental' means 'conveying spiritual strength or refreshment'. Poets and artists of course have made this undeniable: others, not so gifted, experience it at times. In the Church particularly, endued with faith and intent on the approach to God, the sacramental sign has been developed and used with power. The raising of the hand in blessing, the kneeling in prayer, hymns, psalms, pictures, carvings, vestments are symbolic in the true sense of a symbol, namely a known action or object which partakes of the nature of that which it symbolizes. As we have already seen, the symbolism into which we enter and commit ourselves in the Creed is a complete life-scheme. In Holy Matrimony the ring and the joining of hands convey, when they are sincerely used, a special grace for the union beyond what can be achieved by mutual promises. The imposition of hands in Ordination is an active symbol drawing the ordinand into the spiritual fellowship of those who for long centuries have preceded him in ministry, and the gift of the Scriptures is a commissioning for the faithful proclamation of the Word. These are sacramental symbols. The two 'dominical' sacraments need further consideration. Baptism is, at the least, the initiation ceremony of the Christian Church. The water is made an effectual sign of cleansing, and the signing with the Cross an effectual sign of incorporation into the Church. But apart from repentance and assertion of the common faith and willingness of the candidate there is an intention of the Church and a divine command and a personal faith in the case of an adult, and it is these which make the ceremony fully sacramental in conveying through the signs an entry into the power and presence of the Holy Spirit by which the Church lives its corporate life. The effectual grace, or spiritual power thus given is the justification of infant baptism, but in times when so many parents present their children for Baptism without much faith or understanding of their commitment, it may be well that Adult Baptism should become far more common because in it all the elements of infant baptism are present together with personal intention and faith in the candidate. The doctrine of original sin is not now tenable in St. Augustine's sense, nor can penitence be vicarious in the case of an infant.

Baptism is a striking example of the symbol which is activated by the intention of the Church as well as by the divine command, or if Matt. 28. 19 be questioned,[1] by the divine sanction. We have seen that the Christian religion is a symbolic structure created through the perspectives of various ages to 'domesticate', as it were, on earth spiritual realities. These come and have come from God and their expression for man was created or accepted from the past by Jesus Christ in whom God himself was personally active for our salvation. The result has been a framework of belief and practice in which life is made comprehensible and fruitful for good in a spiritual society; we are empowered to live at a level above that of natural humanism by the Holy Spirit. The entry into that society is an uplifting of the personality by the effectual symbol of baptism which implies forgiveness of the past, justification in the present, and new life. The reality in which the symbol partakes is the eternal Spirit whose power since Pentecost is specially present in the Church.

We then turn to the Eucharist. At the Last Supper our Lord used bread and wine as symbols of his human body and blood destined to be offered on the Cross to fulfil his Father's will and to show forth to the world the extent of God's love. He had blessed the symbols to render them no longer to be ordinary but consecrated. He spoke of them as 'my body' and 'my blood' although physically he was present in the upper room. He commanded them to be eaten and drunk as the

[1] The doubt arises not from any technical difficulty, but from doubt whether any Trinitarian formula could have been commanded at a time when baptism in the name of the Lord Jesus was the rule.

closest sign of his spiritual and bodily communion with his followers. Their whole physical nature was to be sacramentally bound to him, and sustained by him by a nourishment which was physical as well as spiritual. Whatever awaited his physical body was in some way to be effectual for their bodies. They were to be bound into some symbolic union with his self-sacrifice, and there was *reality* in the symbol. And, further, the partaking of the consecrated symbol was to be repeated 'in remembrance', and to be a bond of union.

It seems clear that from the first the incipient church made this ceremony central, and regarded it as somehow fulfilling the meaning of Christ's saying 'I am the bread of life.' The service, whether it was incorporated with a love-feast or not, contained an anamnesis or repetition of what he said and did in the upper room. It became quickly a central act of worship for the Christian community; it renewed the sacrificial impulses of Judaism in restoring communion with God; it gave assurance of Christ's continual presence; it expressed thankfulness for his atoning work; and it made a living memorial of his death and resurrection. As a symbol divinely ordained it has been found to be pregnant with many meanings and effective for holiness of life: simple obedience to Christ's command in 'doing' it has been elaborated in ritual, until the Mass has become what Karl Barth called it, a 'religious masterpiece'.

In general, then, the true symbolism of the Christian Faith which is an expression of divine realities and intentions has been made part of man's own 'conversation' in the world by two principal means. The Word, or proclamation of God's will and mercy, sets a standard of life and conduct by divine command which could not be rationally or morally justified on humanistic standards; it permeates the mind and conscience from a divine source. The Sacraments bring the holy life of God to permeate the elements of our natural lives and to sanctify the material, corporeal, and vital aspects of human existence on earth. Both are needed because together they bring man as a whole to God. The Spirit acts through the symbols of word and sacrament to make them means of divine grace. Without some such link the Faith could not become a religion, the city of God could not enter the cities of man.

12

THE LAST THINGS

'I BELIEVE in the resurrection of the body and the life everlasting' (Apostle's Creed).

'I look for the resurrection of the dead, and the life of the world to come' (Nicene Creed).

'At whose coming all men shall rise again with their bodies and shall give account for their own works, and they that have done good shall go into life everlasting and they that have done evil into everlasting fire.' (Athanasian Creed).

Such are our three credal statements about the 'last things'. The Apostle's and Nicene Creeds also refer to our Lord's second coming and his judgment. 'From thence he shall come to judge the quick and the dead' (Apostle's). 'And he shall come again with glory to judge both the quick and the dead: whose Kingdom shall have no end.'

Taken together these statements envisage a return of Christ to earth in glory while there are people still living on it. A rising from the dead of all the departed, in bodily form. A judgment of those who have not died and those who have been raised. A condemnation of sinners to everlasting fire, self-convicted by their own account of their lives. A passing of the righteous to life everlasting in the world to come under the Kingship of Christ.

These prognostications can be amplified by many other statements from the New Testament of unequal evidential value: but taken by themselves they are enough to show how unsatisfactory and incomplete the anticipations of Holy Scripture are. We have an ignoring of the Atonement, a visible descent of Christ from an extra-mundane place, a resurrection of all men as a prelude to judgment, a judgment based on each man's account of his own life, and impossible to conceive, as it would concern untold millions of innumerable religions or none, a fate dependent on ethical conduct only, and everlasting fire for the wicked. 'It may', as Professor A. M. Hunter said, 'be perilous to ignore it': but it is certainly impossible to believe it in any literal sense.

Clearly, if the tenor of this book is accepted, the prophecies must be taken as symbolical of spiritual realities. There is little difficulty for example, for modern Christians in taking the pictures in the book of Revelation as symbolic, and still less in so interpreting other apocalyptic passages in the New and Old Testaments. But clearly credal statements are on a more authoritative level, and their symbols must be carefully scrutinized because their imaginative content is much smaller. They are revelatory, and not pictorial.

These then are as follows: a return of Christ in glory; a bodily resurrection; a judgment; everlasting life; a final Kingdom of Christ, and Hell.

As to the first which we take in connection with 'thy Kingdom come in earth, as it is in Heaven' and the 'new heaven and new earth' and 'the Kingdom of Heaven is ἔντος ὑμῶν' (in the sense 'among you') and which we also read in the light of the 'prophetic foreshortening' of time elements, we may, I believe, conclude a reference to the continual and increasing permeation of human life by the Christ spirit. It is true that at present this permeation may well seem to be a vain hope. Yet it is what all Christians are working for in, be it not forgotten, the *power* of the Holy Spirit. All the calamities and hostilities of our age are news. But beneath them, and to some extent because of them there is an unrecorded ferment: it is partly from general resentment that such things should be, partly from an urge, which is a new and powerful feature of the present age, for sociological improvement, and partly from the increasing sense of responsibility for their neighbours in modern Christendom. 'Religionless Christianity' and the 'outgoing Church' have advanced too far from their base, and are in danger of being cut off from it by the forces of the enemy: but they are a symptom of the coming Kingdom because Christ's social teaching is their inspiration. The challenges of Communism and humanism have produced reactions towards Christian unity and a Christian solution of the enormous social problems of our day, implemented by generous programmes of aid. Young people particularly are seeking in social service an outlet for good instincts which are at present frustrated politically. In fact a certain drift from institutional religious practice is being compensated by a concern for others very much in line with Christ's programme for his Kingdom. The lack of social concern in other religions, when it is realized, will certainly tell in favour of our wider vision. The challenge of Christ burns in the world's conscience.

Of course there is a darker side. 'Wars and rumours of wars' abound: crime increases: moral restrictions have lost their power over non-Christians. Mammon is exercising what is almost a dictatorship, and discontent is rampant. Such conditions are not unforeseen in the New Testament, and its references to them are charged with a sense of their being a prelude to the return of Christ. Whether such prophecies of a cataclysmic prelude to the great event are to be applied to our age must remain doubtful. The horrid possibility of nuclear war cannot be set aside. And yet other ages with their false prophets have cried 'Wolf, Wolf' so often that there are still grounds for hoping that the leaven of the kingdom will work less calamitously, and that Christ may be preached for the whole of mankind before the Kingdom has ripened. Yet the grounds for optimistic humanism and successful evangelism are not so sure as once they seemed.

One point, however, is of importance. The triumphs of Christ have never depended on fear. His victory by cataclysm would abandon most of mankind to ruin. The innocent sufferers would be so multitudinous that the thought of a Kingdom of Christ, so violently inaugurated is abhorrent when there is a credible alternative. And the growth of his Kingdom by a spiritual winning of souls to his way, truth, and life is far more consonant with the record of him who scorned to save himself from the cross by 'ten legions of angels' and who said that it was not his Father's will that one of these little ones should perish.

We may therefore reasonably regard the return of Christ in glory after cataclysmic events to establish his Kingdom as a true symbol of events still future. The reign of Christ is the final triumph of his spiritual government of world affairs. It will come, but only when mankind in general, taught by numerous disasters and false experiments, will learn submission to the law of love and brotherhood. His glory will then shine over all the earth as symbolized in the lightning simile and the coming in the clouds of heaven. Our Lord himself knew not when, nor do we: but Christian discipleship is the leaven, evangelism is the drag-net, and conversion is the buying of the 'pearl of great price'.

The resurrection of the body is a belief rightly founded on the resurrection of our Lord. It has been made clear by innumerable examples that the highest qualities of human personality are untouchable by physical misfortunes. Sometimes the mechanism of the brain becomes disordered and the personal spirit, who uses it as an instrument, fails to find expression. Sometimes spirit and mind become over-involved in the purely physical aspects of our nature and suffer eclipse or partial eclipse. In extreme cases there is little to distinguish the human from the animal: 'they have their reward' which is such as material gratifications can give. The spirit can be quenched: the hope of eternal life may have to be abandoned. But, perhaps more often, the qualities of human persons, which transcend physical satisfactions, are untouchable by sensual or natural decay, even though their expression may become inhibited as the bodily powers weaken. Spiritual personality, in the widest sense, is not dependent on the body, although expressed through a body here.

Now this bodily expression is so closely linked with personality, that it is the means by which we know one another.

We cannot dissociate the person from his body, nor would we wish to. Our friendships and loves depend upon this bodily intercourse, and without it there would be no continuity of persons in an after life. Yet this body decays, dies, disintegrates.

That is one side of the dilemma: the other is that without a body there would be no continuity in knowing one another in the hereafter: and to most people, this alone makes eternal life desirable. A philosopher like Aristotle might be satisfied by an immortality of mind: a saint might look for it and find it in the beatific vision. But philosophers and saints are not very numerous: and less distinguished people would possibly prefer oblivion to an after life which would be utterly new and strange, and have no continuity with their days and hours on earth.

Apart from Kant's deduction of the 'ideas of Reason'—God, freedom and immortality—most Christians are convinced from instinct and from Holy Scripture that God intends for us a future of sinless and timeless happiness after death. This belief points so clearly to a continuity of some kind that the disintegration of our physical bodies must not be considered the obstacle to its justification. Our reception of sense impressions is, as Aristotle says, that which is capable of receiving the perceptible forms without the matter. These forms are transmitted to memory which holds them in a perfection, only dulled by brain processes, ready for revival. It may be this perceptible form which is renewed and active: it may be that memory holds the clue.

Now our memory of ourselves is of quite a different kind from our memories of other people. These latter are objective whereas what we remember of ourselves is subjective—it is of thoughts and feelings which occupied us in situations of people and places which we remember objectively. Speculative though this suggestion may be, it seems as though the restoration of our objective 'form without matter' may be from the memories of those whose happiness requires us to be alive as objects in their world. I have indicated this possible solution already in connection with our Lord's resurrection. The disciples were granted a brief foretaste of the future life in which our Lord as he had become known to and loved by them, was again part of what seemed to be their objective experience.

If our future life depends, under God's providence, on those for whose eternal happiness our lives are necessary, and is recreated from their memories to be objective once more, the present paramount need of people to be cared for, to be loved, to 'count' in other lives would be explained. The ego as a self-regarding unit would die with the body, with all that it has 'taken' for itself from the world: the ego as self-giving would have cast its bread of life upon the waters to receive it again from others, under God's providence 'after many days'.

St. John's vision seems to have penetrated to a similar solution: 'Beloved let us love one another for love is of God: and everyone that loveth is born of God and knoweth God' (1 John 4. 6). 'We know that we have passed from death unto life because we love the brethren' (1 John 3. 16). 'This is my commandment that ye love one another' (John 15. 12).

The stress on mutual love as the secret of eternal life could scarcely be stronger. But we love other things than persons. Places, animals, flowers, work, games, in fact any part of the surround of our lives may be loved so much that our happiness, at least as we estimate it now, would scarcely be complete without them. Here the difference between selfish love and unselfconscious love is of importance: whatever we drag in from the world to gratify ourselves may well perish with the ego as a self-regarding unit. But our *agape* together with that of others who share our unselfish loves may well restore from many memories what has been the material of our present happinesses.

As to final judgment the picture is clearly symbolic. What is its truth apart from the symbol? It is said that Christ will be our judge. In the genuine Christian the spirit of Christ is more or less blended with his personality. In the saint it is almost united to himself. In sinners the consciousness of the Holy Spirit is a continual judgment of their unworthiness, or it may be a continual source of strength. The former aspect predominates in a life which is unchristlike to such a degree that it shrinks away even from the thought of the Spirit's presence or God's knowledge. There could be no clearer indication of the final judgment: it will be self-judgment in the full light of memory by the standards of Christ. All judgment is committed to the Son (John 5. 22). Part of the purpose of his incarnate life was for judgment (John 9. 39). The judgment which was legalistic in the Old Testament, and proclaimed under the same symbol in the New, is to be exercised through our self-condemnation in the light of the perfect manhood of Christ, and in it our hope lies because of his knowledge of our mortal conditions and God's eternal love as shown through him.

The Gospels give us many object lessons by which we can begin our self-judgment here, and by our mortal living mitigate it hereafter. They result in conscience when they are absorbed. For the work of conscience is not only directive (our reason making moral judgments) but also has a minatory and warning effect, and a power of self-condemnation. It is strongest in those who know most of Christ and his ways, but this knowledge is to be sought because its result will be to make the awakening to realities less severe. Self-condemnation now will minimize the loss of our selfish ego hereafter, for self-condemnation is really due to the indwelling spirit. It is possible too that closeness to Christ in this life may even obviate judgment if his words are truly reported by St. John: 'He that heareth my word, and believeth on him that sent me, hath everlasting life, and shall not come into condemnation: but is passed from death unto life' (John 5. 24). The spiritual interpretation of the symbol of the final judgment seems to be true to all its objective aspects, and to remove difficulties in taking them literally which have been great enough to cause many to put the thought aside.

It is generally agreed now that the life everlasting does not mean life going on and on in endless time in a state somewhat like our present one. The terms ἀιώνιος, and in two cases ἀίδιος, both imply timelessness, and are both in common use in the Greek fathers. They mean 'without beginning or end' and both are applied to the after life. Timelessness is to be the character of eternal life.

Time here appears to us mainly as hostile. It shortens joys and lengthens sorrows. It drives us, and binds us: we must come to terms with it for peace of mind. It fools us by anticipation of plenty, and shocks us by ending. It is set by heavenly bodies which seem to perform their ceaseless round unendingly, while our inner sense of 'our' time hastens or dawdles to an ever present expectation of ending. Its uniformity seems to bind our world together, though as we are told by Einstein and others, on the universal scale its uniformity is only for us, and our hours and years are specks in an immensity.

Some have accordingly thought of eternity as an endless 'now': and yet so much of our experience and interest is bound up with change and progress, that life without some kind of time element would be inconceivable except in terms of beatific vision or Nirvana. If history is meaningful to God, as it must be, he cannot be without a time sense pervading his eternal life. It is not duration from which we recoil, but the certainty of ending. Beginning does not trouble us: it only interests. Ending is the trouble. And yet even ending is welcome when trouble comes. The abolition of ending could be terrible as well as happy. It thus appears by a process of exhaustion that eternal life must be characterized by the abolition or negation of evil as its main discernible feature. The realization that evil had ceased to exist, had been completely negated might then be the condition of eternal life. There is ample justification for this in Holy Scripture, and it would be superfluous to enumerate passages. Evil is in its essence negative—absence of good. Its apparent force and vigour in this life is because the absence of good is given a vitality by the potential good or reality with which it is associated. The tragedy of moral evil in a person is given its sting by the potentialities for good which his character possesses. There is no good or evil in the ethical sense in the animal world: there is only a straying of life itself from physical and organic health. In the inorganic world what corresponds to evil is disorder, and this seems to exist as a challenge to man who has the power to order it, and shows this power progressively. The end of evil will be what we call the end of the world, or the coming of the Kingdom of God. After that there will be life without the dread of ending and the corruption which now prevails.

It is scarcely necessary here to answer the objection why should good not be the absence of evil and evil the positive factor. This is pure diabolism and unthinkable.

It has already been made obvious what is symbolized in our belief that Christ will come from Heaven to reign in glory. It is of course closely connected with the spirit of Christ indwelling in the hearts of men, and the final conquest of or fading out of evil into unreality. That this Kingdom will have Christ as its sole ruler and authority is a glorious hope of which the resurrection is a foretaste. Kingdom is a symbol but its essence is easy to understand: evil will not be able to exist under such a rule.

As to Hell; the place of torment for the damned is a piece of vindictive imagination which must be and is being abandoned. Those who have without repentance given themselves to evil are bound to suffer in any future state if they survive. Their self-judgment may be their suffering, and the consciousness of the condemnation of others, if not of God. This may indeed lead to repentance in God's mercy: it may lead to the death-wish and be granted to those who could not endure the glory of the Kingdom: there may indeed be very few of these. But many who have shut out any consciousness of God or of love for any but themselves may well come under the judgment that 'they have had their reward'. Like the wheat at harvest, the tares have had their lives: but they have not borne fruit. No one will have loved these enough to desire to have them as part of his eternity. And yet the love of God is greater than ours and he may have a way. Any living being that has even in this life found satisfaction has not been created in vain, even if, for him or it, this life is all.